RECOLLECTIONS OF MR JAMES LENOX OF NEW YORK AND THE FORMATION OF HIS LIBRARY

A nation's Books are her vouchers; her Libraries are her muniments. *H. S.*

Yours faithfully
Henry Stevens
of Vermont

RECOLLECTIONS OF
MR JAMES LENOX
OF NEW YORK
AND THE FORMATION OF HIS LIBRARY

By HENRY STEVENS of Vermont
Bibliographer and Lover of Books Fellow of the Society of Antiquaries of Old England and Corresponding Member of the American Antiquarian Society of New England of the Massachusetts Historical Society and of the New England Genealogical Society Life Member of the British Association for the Advancement of Science Fellow of the British Archæological Association and the Zoological Society of London Black Balled Athenæum Club of London also Patriarch of Skull & Bones of Yale and Member of the Historical Societies of Vermont New York Wisconsin Maryland &c &c BA and MA of Yale College as well as Citizen of Noviomagus et cetera

LONDON
HENRY STEVENS & SON 115 ST MARTIN'S LANE
Over against the Church of St Martin in the Fields
MDCCCLXXXVI

TO THE READER

WHO faulteth not, liueth not; who mendeth faults is commended: The Printer hath faulted a little: it may be the author oversighted more. Thy paine (Reader) is the least; then erre not thou most by misconstruing or sharpe censuring; least thou be more vncharitable, then either of them hath been heedlesse: God amend and guide vs all.—*Robartes on Tythes* 4° *Camb.* 1613.

FOR AULD LANG SYNE

THESE pages are inscribed with pleasant Recollections of more than forty-five years to my old and valued friend DOCTOR GEORGE H. MOORE

SUPERINTENDENT OF THE LENOX LIBRARY.

PETER FORCE that Eminent Antiquarian of the American Archives brought us together in 1840, and the influence of kindred tastes and pursuits soon wrought an open friendship that has stood the test of years.

In the whirligig of time our orbits have touched but occasionally, yet always with interest, until now he is in charge of many thousands of the rare books that passed through my hands as told in this volume.

LONG MAY HE HAVE CHARGE OF THEM.

Libraries are an index of a nation's, as well as an individual's, wealth, taste, and character. *H. S.*

EXPLANATORY.

IN the spring of 1883, while the Council in London of the Library Association of the United Kingdom were discussing their programme for their Annual Meeting at Liverpool to be held in the fall, I in an unguarded moment told 'the boys,' that they might enter me for a Paper of Recollections of Mr James Lenox or Sir Antonio Panizzi. Our nimble Secretary made a note of it, and accordingly in the first draft——

The foregoing fragment and the Dedication to Dr George H. Moore, were the last lines my father wrote, only a day or two before his lamented decease. The effort of writing

writing was too much for his failing strength, although he retained his mental faculties to the end. The night before his death, he was talking sanguinely of work he proposed to complete in the spring, when he hoped to be better, and he discussed and finally approved of the specimen sheet of this little volume, in the preparation of which he had taken the greatest interest during his illness.

The substance of the following pages formed the subject of a Paper he read with much success at the Liverpool Meeting of the Library Association in September 1883. It was afterwards written out and printed in the Transactions of the Association for that year. In response to numerous suggestions of his friends he had designed to rewrite the Paper on a broader or more general basis with a title 'Forty Years' Reminiscences of a veteran Bibliographer,' or something to that effect. Finding his failing health would not permit him to work up so extensive a subject he then proposed to enlarge this Lenox Paper, and I found in his desk a quantity of memoranda for that purpose. The effort however proving too much for his strength, he consented to let me publish the Paper with only a slight revision, and he intended to explain in the preface that he hoped later on to be well enough to amplify the work in a second edition. The

The Portraits of Mr Lenox and the later one of himself were in the engraver's hands when a day or two before his death he sent for a miniature painted about 1847, which stood in another room, and said 'that portrait should go opposite the chapter on the young man from Vermont.' In deference to that expression of his wish, I have had the earlier portrait engraved as well.

It may not be out of place to mention here that my father has left several Essays on important historical and geographical subjects which I shall hope to publish in course of time.

HENRY N. STEVENS

Public Libraries are intellectual lighthouses for the information and guidance of the people. *H. S.*

Yours very truly
J. Lenox

RECOLLECTIONS OF MR JAMES LENOX OF NEW YORK AND THE FORMATION OF HIS LIBRARY

I

Brief Biographical Sketch by way of Introduction

R JAMES LENOX of New York, the founder of the LENOX LIBRARY in that city, was born in 1800 and died in 1880. A general biography is not aimed at, but only such personal recollections and memoranda respecting him as happen to be in my own private keeping. It is not within my plan to pry into the Lenox preserves,

especially

especially as it is understood that he requested on his death-bed that the private particulars of his life might not be publicly canvassed. This is strictly in accordance with the modest and retiring character of Mr Lenox, and is fully appreciated. Providence however set the Lenox beacon on a hill, and it is too much to expect that death should not have partially removed the bushel that so long obscured it.

For more than a quarter of a century (1845-1871) our intercourse and confidential relations as principal and agent, while he was forming his most valuable library of rare and costly books, were of the closest character, as evidenced by the piles of letters, lists and invoices that passed between us, all still carefully preserved.

Mr Lenox was a man of few words and few intimate friends, but of varied information, much studious reading, extensive correspondence and many books. He was the only

son

son of Robert Lenox, a Scotch merchant who emigrated to New York in 1784, and achieved great wealth during an honourable and long life. James was educated chiefly at Princeton and became a Presbyterian of the strictest sect. He nominally joined his father in business at about the age of twenty-eight as a foreign or importing merchant. The firm was Messrs Robert Lenox & Son at 59 Broadway, and was so styled from 1829 to 1840, when it was changed to 'James Lenox, Merchant' at the same address, and so continued till about 1845. But with his ample fortune and education, Mr James Lenox's mind was rather on music, gems, engravings, paintings, fine arts and literature, than on merchandize. He was most methodical, and had acquired excellent business habits.

On the death of his father in 1840, he inherited almost the whole of the vast Lenox property, including a large farm of some 300

acres

acres in the upper part of the City of New York, which by the year 1865 became surrounded by the rapidly growing city, and in consequence rose to a value of millions. About this time he sold off building lots to the amount of about $3,000,000, reserving some of the largest and best lots for an extensive public hospital, public library and other public enterprises.

Thus we see Mr James Lenox was not only born with a fortune, but Fortune made him her own through life. He was a pattern of industry, method, and good management. He not only himself worked ten hours a-day, but he managed to make his property work for him twenty-four hours daily, accumulating by good investments like rolling snow-balls. He could therefore well afford to do as he liked; and it is well known that he liked to do every thing in his own way, without outside influence, interference or dictation.

Mr

Mr Lenox was ever most generous and charitable, but like my old friend the late Mr George Peabody, the founder of sundry public libraries, he manifested a dislike of being indebted to strangers or neighbours for hints as to his public or private duties; nor would he tolerate any interference in his own charitable impulses. He staked out his own course, hoed his own row, paddled his own canoe and revelled silently in his own generous suggestions, which began literally at home in his own bosom.

He paid his taxes liberally, bore his share of the public burdens, pastured figuratively the widow's cow, helped the needy, but avoided all public offices and politics. Perhaps he carried some of these notions a little too far to be reckoned a good citizen. Were many others to do the same the public weal might suffer; but that is a circumstance hardly to be counted on in New York, where the

the general tendency is rather the other way: too many citizens giving their time and attention to public business, sometimes even to the neglect of their own.

With all this apparent selfishness, Mr Lenox was always studying the welfare of the public, and that of posterity rather than his own. Yet with all his set ways he was ever tolerant in granting to others the same privileges and pleasures of the mind-your-own-business principles and habits which he uniformly assumed and practised for himself. He thought that more young men prospered by minding their own business than by politics or noisy professions. Hence by some he was thought proud, aristocratic, distant and haughty, but those who entertained or expressed such opinions of him manifestly did not know him. To me, who was in constant communication with him for more than a quarter of a century prior to the

founding

founding by charter of the LENOX LIBRARY, he always appeared diffident (almost bashful), simple-hearted, generous, kind, very pious, very retiring and very close-mouthed to outsiders, but as communicative as a child to his intimates; and especially to those in sympathy with his projects and pursuits. With all his amiable qualities none knew his duties better, and knowing them, none dared maintain them more firmly and consistently than he.

Mr Lenox shunned notoriety with the same ardour that others sought it; but when it overtook him, as it frequently did, in spite of his reserve, or when it was blown upon him by the breath of the people, he bore it with Christian fortitude and silence, even avoiding to read the newspapers that heralded his praises, knowing that in most cases the writers communicated only fragments of the truth, often exaggerated and distorted.

His

His love of exactness, or exact conformity to truth, was sometimes carried into inconvenient trifles. He tolerated no interviewers or curiosity hunters, and his own door was seldom opened to visitors except by appointment. He was himself not easily accessible except for good cause, but the treasures of his library, however precious, were generally with great promptitude and courtesy submitted to the use of scholars on due and satisfactory application, but seldom at his own house; nor was he (with rare exceptions) willing to lend his rare books or let them go out of his possession. His frequent practice was to deposit his rarities, when asked for, in the hands of the librarian of the Astor Library, or some similar place of safety, and then by note inform the applicant that the use of the particular book required was at his service there. He was always extremely nervous and fidgety about the safety of his treasures

treasures when out of his own keeping, and uniformly declined applications to 'see his library.' He even refused, among a good many others we know of, Mr Prescott the historian, but at the same time politely informed that distinguished writer that any particular book or manuscript he possessed which Mr Prescott might name should be forwarded for his use *if possible.* The words 'if possible' often used by Mr Lenox in his replies were sometimes incomprehensible, and gave offence to many whose curiosity to see the library overbalanced the desire of access to particular books. The truth was that from about 1845 to 1869 Mr Lenox was actively collecting his library so rapidly, and doing all the work himself, that he had no time to catalogue or arrange his accessions, except a few of the smaller and tidier nuggets which he could put away in the few bookcases in his gallery of art which was also being filled at the same time with paintings and sculpture. The great bulk of his book collections was piled away in the numerous spare rooms of his large house, till they were filled to the ceiling from the further end back to the door, which was then locked and the room for the present done with. The accessions after examination and careful collation, approval and payment, were entered or ticked off in interleaved catalogues of Ternaux-Compans, Rich, Ebert, Hain, Lea Wilson, Offor and others, or in small and special memorandum books, with sufficient clearness for his own use but unintelligible to outsiders. The books were then piled away, or corded up like wood. 'If possible' therefore was a term which Mr Lenox might fairly use, but was not called upon to explain. Indeed I have heard him say that he had often bought duplicates for immediate use or to lend, rather than grope for the copies

copies he knew to be in the stacks in some of his store-rooms or chambers, notably 'Stirling's Artists of Spain,' a high-priced book. Though most tidy and methodical himself he could not permit others to witness this apparent disorder.

One rainy morning in New York, when Mr Lenox and I were discussing 'Nuggets' and telling anecdotes, chiefly of his father and himself, I ventured to ask him if the story I had often heard of his refusing Mr Prescott permission to see his library was true. He replied that it was painfully true. 'I had acquired the Muñoz Manuscripts from Mr Rich and the Lord Steuart de Rothesay Brazilian papers, with many valuable Spanish and Portuguese books from you, and it seemed to be the fashion of every stranger that came to New York to see the Lenox Library. It was very annoying and I thought that a good opportunity to declare myself.' He therefore gave

gave the inquisitive public to understand through Mr Prescott that though he was forming a library it would not be accessible, except on special occasions, till formed. He relaxed his wholesome rules once or twice, particularly in the case of Mr 'Ander Schiffahrt,' but the treatment he received from that distinguished Frenchman was no encouragement to continue to submit to this inconvenience.

As Mr Lenox advanced in years and took upon his shoulders new responsibilities, he felt more and more that his time, his money, and his brains were all his own, in a lower but not a higher sense, they being the three talents specially entrusted to him by a bountiful Providence for use and due increase. So with a conscience as round as his heart, and with a zeal commensurate with his diligence and his knowledge, he plodded on till he had finished all the work he had begun. Like Noah Webster

Webster he was called away in the ripeness of old age just when he had done his life's work, leaving nothing to be finished. A purer, cleaner, and more finished life it is hardly possible to conceive.

Such was JAMES LENOX of New York, who died on the 17th of February 1880, at the age of eighty, the bibliographer, the collector, the founder of one of the most valuable public libraries in the New World, the philanthropist, the builder of churches, the establisher of a large public hospital, the giver to New York of a Home for Aged Women, the dispenser of untold silent charity, and the benefactor of his native city and his honoured country. With all this outcome of a quiet and unostentatious life Mr Lenox was rarely seen of men, and few there be who can from experience divulge the untold particulars of any of his achievements; especially as to how, when and where he accumulated the treasures

sures of the extraordinary library he bequeathed to the public. He was himself content to labour and to wait under the wide-spreading shadow of oblivion, his many virtues bringing to him their own sufficient reward.

This was the man with whom I had the good fortune to exchange commodities for a continued period of twenty-five years. He gave me his money and his friendship, and I sought the world over to supply him with books and manuscripts. If you will overlook the apparent egotism I will now briefly relate how our good genii brought it all about without any fault on the part of either of us. It was to be, and so I suppose it was. I therefore tell the story as history.

II

Yours truly
Henry Stevens
G M B.

II

A young man from Vermont prospecteth in Europe

IN July 1845, a young man from Vermont, at the age of twenty-six, I found myself in London, a self-appointed missionary, on an antiquarian and historical book-hunting expedition, at my own expense and on my own responsibility, with a few Yankee notions in head and an ample fortune of nearly forty sovereigns in pocket. I had contrived by the light of pine knots and dips to pick up some education among the Green Mountains, with a little Latin and less Greek; had passed the

the year 1839 in Middlebury College; 1840 at Washington as a well-paid clerk in the Treasury Department and Senate; 1841-43 in Yale College, where a B.A. degree was won; 1844 in Harvard Law School under Story; all the while dabbling in books and manuscripts by way of keeping the pot boiling. During vacations and holidays I had for five years scouted through the New England and Middle States prospecting in out-of-the-way places for historical nuggets, mousing through public and private libraries and old homestead garrets, chiefly on behalf of Peter Force and his American Archives. From Maine to Virginia many a disused churn, old cradle, dilapidated hencoop, and empty flour barrel had yielded rich harvests of old papers, musty books and sallow pamphlets. These were bought or borrowed and skimmed for Col. Force, while many collectors and librarians enjoyed some pickings. In this

this way the acquaintance of many of the chief authors and book lovers of the country was made; and sufficient experience it was thought had been acquired to try the happier hunting-fields of the Old World, its libraries, its archives, its bookstalls and its old homesteads. It was a wild-goose chase, but as the goose was caught some details may be worth repeating. Those were indeed happy days, when on a July morning one might run down a hundred brace of rare old books on America in London at as many shillings a volume as must now be paid pounds. The shops of Rich, Rodd, Thorpe, Pickering and others were looked through the first fortnight, and books to the amount of more than £1,000 'turned down' and reported to American clients. They were scrambled for in Boston and New York like hot buck-wheat cakes at a College breakfast. It was hardly possible to sweep them together fast enough. The books were sorted, invoiced,

 packed

packed and shipped at Mr Rich's or Mr G. P. Putnam's, and paid for by drafts attached to the bills of lading.

One day in the early autumn of 1845, friend Putnam told me of his executing some orders for a Mr James Lenox of New York, who had recently begun collecting old Bibles, chiefly from Thorpe's catalogues, and said he had bought a few lots in April before from Bright's sale, among them notably a fine copy of Hakluyt, with the rare Mollyneux map, for £25 10*s*. He suggested my offering Mr Lenox some of the nuggets of American history I was collecting. An invoice of about £200 was therefore made by me to Messrs Wiley and Putnam, to which they added a commission of 10 per cent and sent the original direct to Mr Lenox 'on approval.' By return of post every book was ordered except 'Hakluyt's Divers Voyages,' 1582, 4°, at ten guineas, worth £200 now. Mr. Lenox wrote that this was not required, as he already possessed it.

it. This was his first great mistake in book collecting, which he mourned for many a day. Though he wrote by the next fortnightly post to re-order the book, it had been sold and he was years in running down another copy.

The correspondence through Putnam arising out of this blunder led up to other matters. More invoices 'on approval' were sent in the form of 'Messrs Wiley and Putnam, bought of Henry Stevens,' always through Mr Putnam to Mr Lenox, and he ordered almost all lots not duplicate, so that by the end of the year many hundreds of pounds worth had been sent to him, and so a new collector of Americana was launched.

At length, at the beginning of 1846, came a complimentary note from Mr Lenox addressed to me, stating how much pleased he was with these books, and that he was disposed to go on in this new line of collecting, as well as that of Bibles, and inquired if I could not as well ship the books direct

direct to him without the intervention of Mr Putnam, and so save the 10 per cent commission. This was the ostensible reason for the change, but he afterwards told me that a stronger reason for the change with him was not so much the commission, as the fact that the books imported through a large establishment were seen and commented upon by the book fancying gossips of New York, 'who knew so much about his business as no man knew more.' The letter was at once handed over to Mr Putnam with a request to read and answer it, at the same time enclosing my acknowledgment and another invoice. Mr Putnam was of course desirous of retaining so valued a correspondent, explained the situation, and setting forth the advantages of his London and New York agency, solicited a continuance of the triangular arrangement.

During this correspondence I of course remained loyal to friend Putnam

nam, and continued to send reports and bibliographical notes through him, until finally Mr Lenox, finding that there was an unpleasant leakage in New York, wrote me again and direct, intimating his dissatisfaction at the roundabout and expensive mode of proceeding, and declared that he did not at all consider himself tied to Messrs Wiley and Putnam's or any other house as his exclusive London agents; that if I was inclined to continue to correspond with him direct and confidentially, consigning my shipments to himself, I might do so, otherwise the correspondence must cease. As a matter of course Mr Lenox had his own way, as it was his nature to and he could afford to have. For a time this created a shade of coolness between Mr Putnam and myself, but the extent and cordiality of our other relations soon extinguished it. Besides, it was a revelation of a new kind of business with him of which he knew little or nothing.

Thenceforward

Thenceforward for nearly a quarter of a century all Europe was ransacked for bibliographical rarities for Mr Lenox, who indulged in the pleasing satisfaction of being his own confidential importer without feeling called upon to let his intelligent neighbours know how deeply he was putting his hands into his own pockets, or what particular books he was bringing together for the use of their and his own posterity. Our correspondence with lists, invoices and bibliographical notes was frequent and constant, indeed something passing between us by almost every steamer for full fifteen years, until the commencement of the Civil War, when there was a partial suspension of book-hunting on his part for a time.

In thus becoming a correspondent of Mr Lenox it did not square with my notions of fairness to abate a jot of loyalty to Mr John Carter Brown and others who had either given me their orders, or what was more common, had

had indicated in a general way their lines of collecting and desire to participate in the advantages of my opportunities and proclivities. The consequence was that Mr Lenox at first used to complain that he was compelled to submit to a second choice. But he soon learned to appreciate and honour the motives of a foreign agent on whose actions he could count and rely. The truth was that the larger part of the books, maps, prints and manuscripts collected and shipped by me were either 'reported' or sent out 'on approval,' passing round from one client to another till exhausted or returned. Mr Carter Brown for some years in this way enjoyed the first pick, with which he was contented, seldom ordering a book except from a report or auction catalogue. This pre-emption of desiderata was considered of much consequence, but by degrees Mr Lenox got round this difficulty of secondary choice, partially by studying out the bibliography of the subjects

jects most interesting to himself, and ordering in advance what he required. But this could not always be done, because new rarities were constantly turning up that had not been recorded by previous bibliographers. This circumstance added vastly to the interest and importance of my historical and bibliographical mission to the Old World. These remarks, by the way, apply mainly to the materials of the early history and literature of the New World. Other departments further on.

From my knowledge of the general run of the rapidly accumulating collections of Mr Brown, Mr Lenox, and several other less hungry American collectors, I always knew almost to a certainty where to place any 'nugget' that turned up. The world outside of book-hunting may smile at this eagerness for the first choice, but such a smile of pity will most likely vanish away into complaisance on becoming acquainted with the fact that after forty

forty years' experience in sighting and chasing book-rarities, I found that a very large number of the choicest historical and bibliographical nuggets relating to the 'Age of Discovery,' with the exploration and development of the New World, occurred but once in my time, in the market for sale. Happy he who became the winner in such a chase!

III

The 'Mazarine' Bible

S a book collector Mr Lenox was original and peculiar, but nothing could exceed his promptitude, punctuality, energy, exactness, frankness, truthfulness, simplicity and courtesy. He was painfully just and even exacting in having everything in which he participated done in his own way, and when he found himself mistaken, as he not unfrequently did, he always owned up like a man. He used to complain of the hard work of book collecting, and sometimes prayed me not to send him too many books at a time, because it kept him up nights collating, examining,

examining, passing and entering, or ticking them off in his various lists. His interest in every new consignment was intense, and there was no rest until he had cleared his office of every book and remitted a draft in payment. At first he was rather careless about the condition of the copies and cared very little for fine bindings, but by degrees he became acutely quick as to the completeness and purity of his books, until the best bindings that Bedford and Pratt could turn out were not too good or too dear for him. The little plain morocco quartos of Hayday at eight shillings in 1846 grew into works of art eight or ten years later at twenty to forty shillings each. He was an ingrain bibliographer, but his early experience in collecting was not always according to knowledge. He had an eye like a hawk for rare books when he saw them, but was timid in ordering from mere titles in catalogues or reports.

It soon therefore grew into a custom

tom between us that no bargain was complete until he had seen and accepted the book, except when ordered from auction or booksellers' catalogues. This was sometimes rather hard on me, because by far the greater proportion of the many books sent him in this way on approval had to be collected from all parts of Europe, collated, completed if necessary, bound, invoiced and shipped to New York, to await his decision and remittance, consuming in many instances half a year. The disappointments were sometimes as amusing as vexatious, but generally were amicably settled by correspondence. For instance, in early times he ordered from a proof sheet of a Berlin catalogue a tract in German, priced at 115 francs. On receiving it with the price corrected to 15 francs he returned it as 'not wanted,' because he had ordered it under the impression that it was a 'rare book,' as the former price indicated.

Again, when his tastes had grown into

into the mysteries of *uncut* leaves, he returned a very rare early New England tract, expensively bound, because it did not answer the description of 'uncut' in the invoice, for the leaves 'had manifestly been cut open and read.' When it was explained to him that in England the term 'uncut' signified only that the edges were not trimmed, he shelved the rarity with the remark that he 'learned something every day.' On the other hand he kept a great Spanish rarity with margins cut close, because a German youth who desired to practice writing English to me had described it as 'perfect although very closely circumcised.' Our correspondence and intercourse were full of innocent surprises of this sort, but perhaps showing too much frankness and simplicity to be repeated in print.

Mr James Lenox was always liberal and even willing if necessary to pay a high price for a very rare book, provided he was sure the transaction was open

open and perfectly fair, but he was ever suspicious of paying more than the market value. A curious case occurred in 1847, some eighteen months after I had begun supplying him with Americana and occasionally with other rare books. I had announced to him among other bibliographical gossip that a fine and perfect copy of the forty-two line Latin Bible of 1450-1455, usually but unjustly called the 'Mazarine' Bible, was soon coming on for sale by auction at Sotheby's, and, though a copy had been sold as high as £190, suggested that he should go in for it at that or even a higher price if necessary. I gave a careful collation and description of the two volumes, and stated that though both Mr Putnam and I would probably be absent in Paris at the time of the sale, his order would be attended to by the house of Messrs Wiley and Putnam, to whom he was requested to address his orders and instructions. His order came during our absence, with a simple

simple request to the manager to buy the Bible for him, without any particular instruction or limit as to price. Mr Davidson the manager was thus unexpectedly thrown on his 'discretion,' and he, it seemed to me afterwards, wisely decided to exercise that virtue by buying the book against all comers, and accordingly he attended the sale personally and ran the book until it was knocked down to Messrs Wiley and Putnam at £500, at that time pronounced to be a 'mad price,' though other copies have since been sold by auction at from £1,600 to near £4,000.

This 'mad price' was at once heralded as such in the London papers, and the book was stated to have been bought by a well-known American collector against Sir Thomas Phillipps, under exciting circumstances. Sir Thomas had arranged with Messrs Payne and Foss, after his peculiar manner, to buy the Bible for him at an agreed limit of £300. But Sir Thomas

Thomas was so anxious about the result that he committed the indiscretion of going to the sale rooms himself to witness the competition. When the biddings between Mr Davidson and Mr Foss had exceeded £300, Sir Thomas, when he could not induce Mr Foss to go on, took up the competition himself, and ran his American opponent up to £495, when Mr Foss arrested his mad career, and the hammer fell at Mr Davidson's final bid of £500 for Messrs Wiley and Putnam.

That sale was a bibliographical event, and was greatly talked and written about both in London and New York, insomuch that Mr Lenox, whose name as that of the unlucky purchaser had been freely used, declined to clear the book from the New York Custom House, and pay for it. The cost, including the commission, expenses and the customs duty, amounting to about $3,000, was deemed by him an amount of

indiscretion

indiscretion for which he could not be responsible. However, after some reflection and a good deal of correspondence, he took home the book, and soon learned to cherish it as a bargain and the chief ornament of his library. Mr Putnam soon after returned to America, and the result of this campaign was all in my favour.

Mr Lenox used often to pay an unprecedentedly high price for a prime rarity, with the remark that he 'could at present find the five pound notes more easily than such books, but you must not tell anybody how much I have paid.' A few years later, when I quoted the same books at two to four times the prices he paid, he willingly removed the injunction of secrecy.

IV

'*The Wicked Bible*'

MR LENOX was so strict an observer of the Sabbath that I never knew of his writing a business letter on Sunday but once. In 1855, while he was staying at Hôtel Meurice in Paris, there occurred to me the opportunity one Saturday afternoon, June 16, of identifying the long lost octavo Bible of 1631, which has the negative omitted in the Seventh Commandment, and purchasing it for fifty guineas. No other copy was then known, and the possessor required an immediate answer. However I raised some points of inquiry and obtained permission to hold

hold the little sinner and give the answer on Monday. By that evening's post I wrote to Mr Lenox and pressed for an immediate reply, suggesting that this prodigal though he returned on Sunday should be housed. Monday brought a letter 'to buy it,' very short but tender as a fatted calf. On June 21 I exhibited the volume at a full meeting of the Society of Antiquaries of London, at the same time nicknaming it 'The WICKED BIBLE,' a name that has stuck to it ever since though six copies are now known.

In the Proceedings of the Society, vol. iii. page 213, appeared this record: 'Henry Stevens, Esq. F.S.A. exhibited an octavo Bible of the authorized version, called "The Wicked Bible" from the circumstance of its being filled with gross and scandalous typographical errors, not the least remarkable of which is the omission of the important word *not* in the Seventh Commandment, leaving it to read *Thou shalt commit adultery.* Upon

Charles

Charles I. being made acquainted with the fact by Archbishop Laud, the King's printers, Robert Barker and Martin Lucas, were summoned before the Star Chamber, and on the fact being proved were fined in the sum of £300, and the entire edition of 1,000 copies was ordered to be destroyed. Although the book has been diligently sought after for the last hundred years, no copy has hitherto been known to have been discovered; and though many writers have told the story for the last two hundred years, no one identified the edition or indicated the year in which it was printed. The present volume settles the question. It was printed by the Royal Printers in 1631, in octavo. The present copy is believed to be unique. It came from Holland within the last few days and is on its way to America. It cost its present owner fifty guineas.'

In the discussion that followed I ventured to assure the Society that though

though the Commandment was actually so printed by the King's printers, I felt sure that it was not now binding on the Fellows of the Society of Antiquaries. Lord Macaulay was present at that meeting, but did not at first credit the genuineness of the typographical error. Lord Stanhope however, on borrowing the volume, convinced him that it was the true wicked error.

As this 'Wicked Bible' has attracted a good deal of attention since 1855, and has led certain serious and learned critics called divines into historical and bibliographical errors, it may not be uninteresting to name a few particulars respecting it. The volume, comprising the Book of Common Prayer, the Genealogies, the Bible and the Psalms in Metre, all bound in one and as clean and fresh as new, had been the property of the celebrated John Canne while he resided in Holland, and was left in a library founded by him. It was offered to me me as '*unique*' and priced accordingly, with the assurance that no abatement would be made. On taking it home to my house in Camden Square that Saturday night and overhauling my pile of octavo Bibles laid aside for collation and binding, I was both delighted and disappointed to find that I was already the possessor of a 'Wicked Bible,' an overlooked duplicate of the copy offered, though not so 'unique as my other copy,' as my old American friend Dowse used to say, for it contained the Bible only, in inferior condition and wanting twenty-three leaves in the Psalms.

On Monday morning, when the owner came for his Bible or the fifty guineas, I showed him my copy in triumph, to convince him that his was not unique and hence was not worth the price asked. He at once admitted my plea and accepted £25. My junior copy, after being done up in forel, was sold in the autumn of 1855 to Mr Panizzi for eighteen guineas,

guineas, and is now in the British Museum, locked up in Case 24. a. 41, bearing the stamp of Jan. 3 1856, when paid for. Mr Winter Jones was afterwards fortunate enough to procure the twenty-three missing leaves for five guineas from the Rev Mr Jennings, who had picked up a copy wanting three leaves for which he asked twenty guineas, so that the Museum copy is also complete. Mr Jennings sold the remainder of his copy, which then wanted twenty-six leaves, for fifteen guineas to Mr Francis Fry of Bristol, who I believe succeeded in completing it and sold it to Dr Bandinel for the Bodleian Library. It was lent to the Caxton Exhibition of 1877, where it attracted more attention than any honest Bible of the Collection. A fourth copy is preserved in the Euing Library in Glasgow, and a fifth fell into the hands of Mr Henry J. Atkinson of Gunnersbury, in 1883. In the autumn of 1884 a sixth copy,

copy, which might be designated the Godiva copy, was brought to me for identification by a gentleman of Coventry, who said it had recently been picked up in Ireland. Thus you see in less than thirty years this *unique* has increased and multiplied like lost sinners.

The truth seems to be that few books remain 'unique' long, when their attractions have been once noised abroad. Immediately on completing the purchase I wrote to Mr George Offor announcing my bibliographical luck, and he replied the next day, June 18, 'What a world this would be if such Bibles abounded! Thank goodness they are so rare that their existence has been doubted and disbelieved. I and my father before me sought it for sixty years *diligently* as Herod sought the young Child, and like him could not find it. Nor can I yet fully believe its genuineness, but hope soon to be cured of my unbelief, for seeing is is believing.' A sight of the volume was his 'convincement.'

Like the early translators this Bible sought a refuge in Holland, where it escaped the flames, more fortunate than Tyndale or Rogers. Of the six copies now known, this one preserved in the 'Lenox Library,' New York, is by far the purest and finest, if not the wickedest of all; and I never heard that Mr Lenox ever felt or expressed any compunctions of conscience for having ordered it on a Sunday. It should perhaps be stated that the Germans have also their 'Wicked Bible' of precisely like tenor, only as in many other things the Germans are a hundred years behind the English. They are however, I believe, as yet limited to the possession of a single copy, which is carefully guarded in the quaint old library of Wolfenbüttel, where I recently had the sinful pleasure of seeing, handling and collating it. The wicked typographical error consists as in its English namesake in dropping the negative. It is a little decimosexto volume in small German black letter, double columns, in a form not quite so large as the English, and has this title :—'BIBLIA/ Dasist/ Die gantze/ Heil Geschrift/ Altes und Neues/ Testaments./ Nach der Teutschen Ubersetzung/ D. Martin Luther/ . . . . Nebst der Vorrede/ Des. S. Her Baron E. H. von Caustein./ Die XXXIV Auflage./ *Halle*, Zu finden in Maÿsenhause MDCCXXXI' Exodus xx. 14. 'Du solt ehebrechen.' We are not aware if the French have a like authority.

V

Voyages and Travels. Bunyans. Miltons. Shakespeares

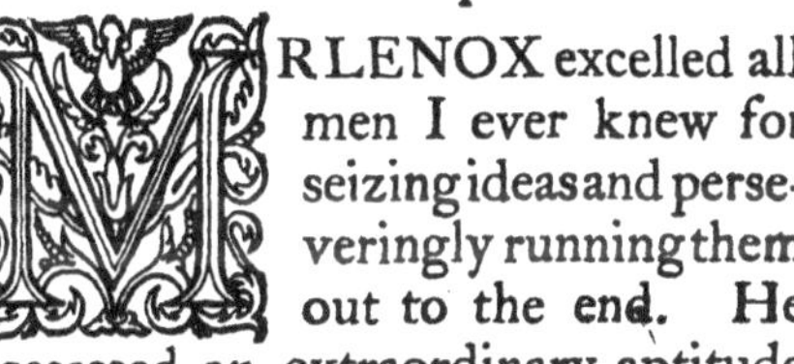

MR LENOX excelled all men I ever knew for seizing ideas and perseveringly running them out to the end. He possessed an extraordinary aptitude for sticking to and finishing up any work he had in hand. This however, I fancy, was one of the virtues that was not in all cases its own reward. His first absorbing penchant was for collecting early editions of the Bible and parts thereof in all languages. Then he took to books relating to North and South America, including all the great collections of voyages and travels, as well as the prior or

original

original editions of which they were composed. This soon led to collecting everything pertaining to the great 'Age of Discovery,' whether in Spanish, Portuguese, English, French, Dutch, Italian or German. In this way he soon had more pet-lambs than he could well watch, such as De Bry, Hulsius, Ramusio, Purchas, Thevenot, Haertgerts, Saeghman, etc. Then there were all the editions, translations, and variations of Columbus, Vespucci, Marco Polo, Mandeville, Varthema, Peter Martyr, Enciso, Las Casas, Cortes, Oviedo, Gomara, Cieza, Xeres, etc., etc.

Besides these he took very early to his favourite author John Bunyan, and not only edited an edition of the 'Pilgrim's Progress,' but undertook to collect all editions and translations of it. In this he was particularly successful, having eventually acquired nearly every one of the early English editions of parts I, II, and III, as numbered from the 1st to the 32nd.

No

No collection known can be compared with his, that of the late Mr Offor being in no way equal to it. Indeed for nearly twenty years I carried in my pocket lists of the editions of the P.P. he had, as well as those known ones he wanted, and in that way catered earnestly, allowing nothing to slip through my fingers that it was possible to secure for him. In reading catalogues and reports from all parts of the world, one eye at least was always kept peeled for his desiderata.

In the same manner he undertook to bring into his net all the editions of Milton, and succeeded in acquiring it is believed nearly all the known editions, as well as many not previously recognized, of the early separate pieces in both prose and verse of the author of 'Areopagitica' and 'Paradise Lost.' Indeed his collection of Miltons excels that of the British Museum and that of the Bodleian put together, rich as those libraries are in Miltons.

This

This mode of collecting has certainly its advantages, but it can hardly be denied that it is attended with serious disadvantages. The result of all Mr Lenox's enormous study and labor, to say nothing of his vast expenditure, it must be confessed is a 'patchy library' as he left it. His favorite subjects and authors he rendered astonishingly rich for a period of only thirty-five years research; but the subjects and authors he totally neglected at the same time are also astonishingly numerous. The verdict of posterity however will probably be that he acted well his part, leaving to others the others' parts. Three or four more lives like his would render the Lenox Library an all-round public library.

It is impossible in these brief recollections to go over regularly the records of our correspondence from 1845 to 1873, but I may say that 1854 and 1855 were very busy years with both of us. As caterer for him

I expended in these two years alone more than fifty thousand dollars; many opportunities occurring then that can hardly ever occur again for any collector of Mr Lenox's tastes. On reviewing the invoices of these two years, I am confident that if the same works were now to be collected, they would cost more than two hundred and fifty thousand dollars. But can such and so many rare books ever be collected again in that space of time? A large part of 1855-56 Mr Lenox spent in Europe and picked up rare books wherever he met with them, but I speak only of my own relations with him, though he generally kept me posted in his accessions, especially in those subjects already mentioned.

He had set his heart on 'the four folios,' and by changing and chopping about, besides having secured the famous Baker copy, he had secured nearly all the variations known, including all the variations of the

third

third folio of 1663. But I could never induce him to invest in the Shakespeare quartos until December 1855. I then offered him, while he was still in Paris, in one lump about forty of the quartos, all in good condition and some of them very fine, for £500, or including a fair set of the four folios, for £600. This offer upset his previous resolutions, and he bought the whole, thus becoming at one step, the possessor of perhaps the finest Shakespearian collection then in private hands.

An exact list of the quartos will enable an expert to judge of the prices compared with what such a collection would bring now. They were, Merry Wives, 2nd and 3rd editions, 1619 and 1630; Midsummer Night, 2nd, Roberts 1600; Love's Labor's Lost, 2nd, 1631; Merchant of Venice, 1st, 2nd, 3rd and 4th editions, 1600, 1600 Roberts, 1637, 1652; Taming of the Shrew, 1st edition, 1631; Richard II,

4th

4th and 5th editions, 1615, 1654; Henry IV, 2nd, 5th and 8th editions, 1599, 1613, 1639; Henry V, 3rd edition, 1608; Richard III, 4th, 7th and 8th editions, 1612, 1629, 1634; Romeo and Juliet, 5th edition, 1637; Macbeth, 1st edition, 1674; Hamlet, 4th and 7th editions [1607], 1637; Lear, 1st and 3rd editions, 1608, 1655; Othello, 1st, 2nd and 3rd editions, 1622, 1630, 1655; Pericles, 3rd and 5th editions, 1619, 1635; Henry VI, 2nd part, 4th edition [1619], and 3rd part, 3rd edition [1619]; Sir John Oldcastle, 1600; Lord Cromwell, 1602, unique; Yorkshire Tragedy, 1619; Rape of Lucrece, 16mo, 1616; Birth of Merline, 1662; The Puretaine, 1607; The London Prodigal, 1605; and two or three others, besides the four folios, all for £600! He was greatly pleased with his bargain, but I could never tempt him to go further in the Shakespeare quartos.

VI

Mr Lenox buys a 'Turner'

IT is to be borne in mind that Mr Lenox was not merely a book collector. He was a good citizen and excellent neighbour, fulfilling his duties in all situations. The large hall in his new house, 53 Fifth Avenue, was constructed rather as a Gallery of Art than a Library, though adapted to both. This brings to mind a characteristic anecdote, which I often heard Mr C. R. Leslie, the Royal Academician, relate of his two friends Mr Lenox and Mr Turner his brother Academician. Mr Leslie, about 1847 I think, received a letter covering a sight draft on Barings,

requesting

requesting him to be so good as to purchase of his friend Mr Turner the best picture by him he could get for the money, giving directions for the shipment to New York.

With draft in pocket Mr Leslie called on the distinguished artist, and told him frankly that he had called to purchase one of his pictures for an American friend. 'I have no picture to sell to your American friend,' was the grumpy reply. 'But surely,' answered Mr Leslie, who understood the humour of the artist, 'out of so many one might very well be spared for New York.' 'No, my pictures are not adapted to American taste or American appreciation of Art. You had better apply to Mr Soand-so, if you require a picture suitable for the gallery of an American,' and then commented severely on America and Americans, their refinement, their money-grubbings, and their knowledge of Art. Finally Mr Leslie, all the while well knowing that Mr

Mr Turner at that time was desirous of selling his pictures and at reasonable prices too, said, 'Well, Mr Turner, you are in this matter mistaken I assure you, for I have been connected as an Art teacher with the Military Academy of West Point, and am tolerably well acquainted with the Art characteristics of that growing country. Besides I well know Mr Lenox, and am sure a picture of yours could not find a better home on either side of the Atlantic. You are too suspicious; you need run no risk from him or me, I have nothing more to say or do. Here is Mr Lenox's letter and draft for £800 which you may encash at Barings to-day. Pray select such a picture as will in your own judgment do yourself the most credit in the Art-benighted country you decry.'

This speech or the letter or the draft fetched up the artist, and he promptly confessed that some good might

might come even out of New York; so he at once turned round a small picture standing on the floor against the wall and said, 'There, let Mr Lenox have that, one of my favorites; he is a gentleman, and I retract: will that suit you, Mr Leslie?' 'I am unwilling to take any responsibility, Mr Turner, in the selection; if the painting satisfies you, and you recommend it at that price, I will endorse the draft to you and take the picture away with me.' And that was the way Mr Lenox won his first 'Turner.'

But this is not the end of the story. The painting soon after arrived in New York, was cleared from the Custom House and delivered in Fifth Avenue only a few minutes before the closing of the fortnightly mail for England. Mr Lenox therefore had time only to hastily acknowledge its receipt safe and in good condition. He had, he wrote, caught only a glance at the picture, but

but he could not help adding that that glance disappointed him. On receiving this curt and scarcely courteous letter, Mr Leslie said he resolved thenceforward to abstain from executing responsible commissions for friends. By the following mail two weeks later came a second letter from Mr Lenox, the substance of which was, 'Burn my last letter, I have now looked *into* my "Turner" and it is all that I could desire. Accept best thanks.' In telling the story Mr Leslie used sometimes parenthetically and facetiously to remark, 'I suppose Mr Lenox, like some others who view "Turners" for the first time, somehow got the picture bottom side up.'

VII

VII

'*The Bay Psalm Book*'

IN our pecuniary relations Mr Lenox was so methodical, prompt and perfectly honest that I grew into the habit of relying too much upon his statements and 'footings' of our accounts. He made mistakes as well as I, but in his case, as he used to say, they were fortunately almost wholly against himself. He had a particular horror of any blunder that was in his own favour. Once in New York, after we had settled up a long and intricate account with many exchanges and choppings, which could not be settled by letter, and I had received

received a pretty large cheque and invested it in a bill of exchange on London at a time when I was hard pressed for ready money, I was surprised one morning before breakfast by receiving a note from him announcing that he had discovered a dreadful mistake in our settlement, and requesting me to call upon him at nine o'clock. It spoiled my breakfast, for I felt sure that I should be called upon to disgorge. While the clock was striking nine I pulled his bell and was promptly admitted. 'Oh,' said he, 'I thought of that horrid mistake in bed last night, and have hardly been able to sleep since; pray pardon me, I cannot think how I came to do so stupid a thing; here is another cheque for five hundred dollars for that Bible.' I was relieved and could have hugged him, but as that was not his way I quietly observed that I had not yet noticed the error, simply adding, after the manner of Mr Toots, that it was 'of no consequence.'

consequence.' I promised to forgive him, and returned to the Clarendon with an improved appetite for breakfast.

For nearly ten years Mr Lenox entertained a longing desire to possess a perfect copy of 'THE BAY PSALM BOOK,' the New England metrical version of the Psalms printed by Stephen Daye at Cambridge, N.E. 1640, the first book printed in what is now the United States. He gave me to understand that if an opportunity occurred for securing a copy for him I might go as far as one hundred guineas. Accordingly from about 1847 till his death, six years later, my good friend William Pickering and I put our heads and book-hunting forces together to run down this rarity.

The only copy we knew of on this side the Atlantic was a spotless one in the Bodleian Library, which had lain there unrecognized for ages, and even in the printed catalogue of 1843

 its

its title was recorded without distinction among the common herd of Psalms in verse. The book bears no name of place or printer, the imprint being simply 'Imprinted 1640.' I had handled it several times with great reverence and noted its many peculiar points, but, as agreed with Mr Pickering, without making any sign or imparting any information to our good and obliging friend Dr Bandinel, Bodley's Librarian. We thought that when we had secured a copy for ourselves, it would be time enough to acquaint the learned Doctor that he was entertaining unawares this angel of the New World.

Under these circumstances, therefore, only an experienced collector can judge of my surprise and inward satisfaction, when on the 12th January 1855, at Sotheby's, at one of the sales of Pickering's stock, after untying parcel after parcel to see what I might chance to see, and keeping ahead of the auctioneer, Mr Wilkinson,

kinson, on resolving to prospect in one parcel more before he overtook me, my eye rested for an instant only on the long lost Benjamin, clean and unspotted. I instantly closed the parcel, (which was described in the Catalogue as Lot '531 Psalmes other Editions, 1630 to 1675 black letter, a parcel,') and tightened the string, just as Alfred came to lay it on the table. A cold-blooded coolness seized me, and advancing towards the table behind Mr Lilly I quietly bid in a perfectly neutral tone 'sixpence,' and so the bids went on increasing by sixpences until half-a-crown was reached and Mr Lilly had loosened the string. Taking up this very volume he turned to me and remarked that 'This looks a rare edition, Mr Stevens, don't you think so? I do not remember having seen it before,' and raised the bid to five shillings. I replied that I had little doubt of its rarity, though comparatively a late edition of the Psalms, and

and at the same time gave Mr Wilkinson a sixpenny nod. Thenceforward a 'spirited competition' arose between Mr Lilly and myself, until finally the lot was knocked down to 'Stevens' for nineteen shillings! I then called out, with perhaps more energy than discretion, 'delivered.' On pocketing this volume, leaving the other seven to take the usual course, Mr Lilly and others inquired with some curiosity, 'What rarity have you got now?' 'Oh nothing,' said I, 'but the first English book printed in America.' There was a pause in the sale, while all had a good look at the little stranger. Some said jocularly, 'there has evidently been a mistake, put up the lot again.' Mr Stevens, with the book again safely in his pocket, said, 'Nay, if Mr Pickering, whose cost mark of γ [3*s*] did not recognize the prize he had won, certainly the cataloguer might be excused for throwing it away into the hands of the right person

son to rescue, appreciate and preserve it. I am now fully rewarded for my long and silent hunt of seven years.'

On reaching Morley's I eagerly collated the volume, and at first found it right with all the *usual* signatures correct. The leaves were not paged or folioed. But on further collation I missed sundry of the Psalms, enough to fill four leaves. The puzzle was finally solved when it was discovered that the inexperienced printer had marked a sheet with the signature w after v, which is very unusual.

This was a very distressing disappointment, but I held my tongue, and knowing that my old friend and correspondent, George Livermore of Cambridge, N.E., possessed an imperfect copy, which he and Mr Crowninshield, after the noble example of the 'Lincoln Nosegay,' had won from the Committee of the 'Old South,' in Boston, together with another

other and perfect copy, I proposed an advantageous exchange, and obtained the four missing leaves. Mr Crowninshield strongly advised Mr Livermore against parting with his four leaves, because, as he said, 'they would enable Stevens to complete his copy, and place it in the library of Mr Lenox, who would then crow over us because he also had a perfect copy of the Bay Psalm Book.'

Having thus completed my copy and had it bound by Francis Bedford in his best style, I sent it to Mr Lenox for £80. Five years later I bought the Crowninshield Library in Boston for $10,000, mainly to obtain his perfect copy of the Bay Psalm Book, and brought the whole library to London. This second copy, after being held several months, was at the suggestion of Mr Thomas Watts, offered to the British Museum for £150. The Keeper of the Printed Books however never had the courage to send it before the Trustees

for

for approval and payment; so after waiting five or six years longer the volume was withdrawn, bound by Bedford, taken to America in 1868, and sold to Mr George Brinley for 150 guineas. At the Brinley sale in March 1878, No. 847, Part I, it was bought by Mr Cornelius Vanderbilt for $1,200, or more than three times the cost of my first copy to Mr Lenox. The British Museum still lacks the first book printed in New England.

VIII

VIII

The Drake Map. Aratus' Phaenomena. The Forged Tyndale Manuscript

IN October 1849, there occurred for sale at Sotheby's a very rare copper-plate map of the World, represented in two hemispheres, engraved by Hondius, and published by him at Amsterdam about 1595. On each side and below it were pasted broad columns of text in Dutch, taken chiefly from Hakluyt and Linschoten. There were also inserted in the text fine copper-plate portraits of Drake and Cavendish, and on the map were traced the routes of those two celebrated

brated circumnavigators. The whole sheet measured about 37 by 25 inches. I had resolved to secure this unique geographical gem for Mr Lenox, and, as was my general custom at that time, gave my order, under a mistaken notion of economy, to a celebrated bookseller who undertook to buy for me at sales at a small commission, drawing upon me at short sight as fast as the purchases amounted to £50 or so, he paying the auctioneers, as he could arrange, sometimes months later. For this map I gave a limit of 50 guineas. It was however bought by him for another order for something under 30 guineas, and immediately delivered. When I came to enquire into the matter a cock-and-bull story was told me about a mistake between his clerk and the auctioneer, which on being run out proved to be not so much the truth as the other thing. So after that I kept my auction orders to myself and executed my own com-

 missions,

missions, greatly to my own advantage. In this way Mr Lenox and I lost the Drake, but we gained in confidence and experience. I was afterwards glad to find that the map was bought for the British Museum, where one could use it as freely as if it were his own. This proved a valuable lesson, both to self and correspondents, having taught me severely while acting as confidential agent never to intrust important, or even trifling, commissions to a third party, however honest and plausible. 'Close mouths catch no flies.' It is a great mistake to imagine you are going to get your books cheaper in the long run by intrusting your commissions to a bookseller who threatens to oppose you unless you buy off his opposition by giving him your orders. Thorpe failed in this manœuvre as others have conspicuously done since. They may get the lots, but are pressed in the chase into giving often more than necessary.

Shortly

Shortly after, in 1850, there occurred for sale at the same auction rooms a copy of 'Aratus' Phaenomena,' Paris 1559, in 4° with a few manuscript notes and this autograph signature on the title "Jo. Milton, Pre 2*s* 6*d* 1631." This I thought would be a desirable acquisition for Mr Lenox, and accordingly I ventured to bid for it as far as £40 against my late opponent for the Drake Map, but he secured it at £40 10*s*, remarking that 'Mr. Panizzi will not thank you for thus running the British Museum.' 'That remark,' I replied, 'is apparently one of your gratuities. Mr Panizzi is, I think, too much a man of the world to grumble at a fair fight. He has won this time, though at considerable cost, and I am sure Mr Lenox will be the first to congratulate him on securing such a prize for the British Museum.' 'I did not know that you were bidding for Mr Lenox.' 'It was not necessary that you

you should.' 'Perhaps at another time,' said he, 'we may arrange the matter before-hand so as not to oppose each other.' 'Very well,' I replied, 'if you will bring me a note from Mr Panizzi something to this effect: "Mr Stevens, please have a knock-out with the bearer, the agent of the British Museum, on lot * * and greatly oblige Mr John Bull and your Obd[t] Servant, A. P.," I will consider the proposition, and if Mr Lenox or any other of my interested correspondents is not unwilling to combine or conspire to rob or cheat the proprietors, the "thing" may possibly be done. Meanwhile until this arrangement is concluded let us hold our tongues and pursue an honest course.' That man never again suggested to me to join him in a 'knock-out.'

On the 27th of June 1865, there was sold at Sotheby's, in Mr George Offor's sale, lot '193 Portions of the New Testament, translated from the Greek

Greek into English by that noble and venerable martyr William Tyndale, in his own handwriting, and accompanied by his own drawings in 1502.' This handsome volume, elaborately bound by C. Murton, had often been shown to me by Mr Offor as the 'Pearl of his Collection.' He apparently himself had no doubt of its genuineness and authenticity, and in the prolegomena of Bagster's Hexapla had himself so described it. Anderson however in his Annals, II, Appendix iii, ridiculed this idea, and suggested 1562 instead of 1502 as the date of the MS. In the auction catalogue nearly a page is devoted to the volume, setting forth Mr Offor's claims and the various reasons why it should be regarded a forgery, with this *caveat emptor* the lot 'must be purchased on the buyer's own judgment as to its being genuine or not.' The paper is undoubtedly older than 1502, but the 27 drawings are copies, some of them, of well-known well-known pictures of later date. Mr Offor valued the volume at £300, a considerable price in his day. It was bought in for the Offor family for £31.

After the first two out of the eleven days' sale, and before scarcely any of the lots had been cleared, Sotheby's premises were burnt out, including, among many other collections, the whole of the Offor Library. The Offor salvage, burnt, wet and scorched, was bought by me for £300, including this 'Tyndale' little damaged, except that the 'antique oak cover' was somewhat smoked, warped and injured, but all was easily restored. On careful and critical examination the volume was pronounced and treated as a forgery, not of 1562 but of the present century. What then was to be done with it? The MS. had got itself into history, and had become an authority, spurious or genuine. To destroy it would only be lending aid to to those who believed in its genuineness, while its opponents would be deprived of the best evidence of the forgery, the book *de visu.*

Under these circumstances, after having offered it at a small price to the British Museum, the Bodleian and Mr Francis Fry without success, I sent it to Mr Lenox as a rank forgery, and submitted to him the necessity, for the sake of truth, of preserving it carefully as a warning. He agreed with me in this suggestion and purchased the volume for the Lenox Library at £25. It was agreed that it should be branded for ever as a forgery, of no historical or critical value whatever. Now what is the subsequent history of that remarkable volume? Mr Lenox died in 1880, having apparently forgotten to brand the outcast. More recently a German scholar, now residing in New Jersey, while searching for materials respecting William Tyndale has turned up this rejected but preserved

served pretender, and in his new edition of Tyndale's Pentateuch, pp. lvi-lix, has very minutely described it in four large pages, thus giving it an importance and prominence it has no right to, and which abler, honester and more accurate writers will find it hard hereafter to combat.

Dr Mombert, it is true, in quoting Anderson and Westcott showing that these writers regarded the work as spurious, casts a doubt over its authenticity, making a fair show of research, but he fails altogether to put his foot firmly down on the imposition. He ought in my judgment to have omitted noticing it altogether, or have pronounced the verdict of a scholar and historian. He has merely scotched the serpent and not strangled it, a great injustice to Mr Lenox and the Lenox Library. This slip-shod bibliography in history is, I am sorry to say, becoming the fashion in New York and Boston. Would-be historians and 'narrative'

writers

writers are industriously picarooning and compiling 'history' by stringing together an ostentatious show of discordant authorities, relevant, irrelevant and contradictory, leaving the victimized reader to draw his own conclusions, because as historians they either are not able to form a sound opinion, or dare not express it.

IX

The Dati Columbus and Hariot's Virginia

WITHIN two years of his entering on the great project of collecting rare books relating to America, Mr Lenox became very desirous of possessing a good and perfect copy of 'Virginia's First Folio,' that is, Thomas Hariot's 'Briefe and true Report of the new found land of Virginia,' published in English, with copper-plate engravings by Theodore De Bry at Frankfort in 1590, after John White's drawings. I had already provided Mr John Carter Brown with a fine copy, but led Mr Lenox

Lenox to believe that even London could not be relied upon for another copy of so rare and important a book in the same decade.

But an opportunity occurred sooner than could have been counted on. One morning in June 1847, while walking down the King's Library, I saw approaching, Mr Panizzi with his friend Sir David Dundas. When we approached within about ten yards, Mr Panizzi stopped and said, with arms a-kimbo and a most quizzical face, 'Tell me Mr Stevens, have you seen Mr Libri's catalogue?' 'Yes,' I replied. 'Are you going to buy for your friend Mr Lenox the Dati Columbus?' 'Yes, since you ask me the direct question, that is my intention, and I answer you frankly; though I am not in the habit of telling my right hand what my left is going to do. I have not yet received a specific order, but I know Mr Lenox's drift.' 'Very well,' he said. 'It is between us three, and you may speak

speak frankly ; but you really must not buy that Columbus Letter in Italian against the British Museum. Now that we have the Grenville Columbuses, with the others we had before, the library possesses, I believe, all the known editions except the Paris one you showed me before you sent it to your friend Mr Brown. I ought not to miss acquiring this for many reasons, and therefore I ventured to put this blunt question in the presence of Sir David.' Then Sir David said, 'Certainly the British Museum ought to secure this little book at any price in reason. What do you think it will go for?' I replied, 'Probably from £50 to £100, perhaps more, it being four leaves, unique, and well bound.' 'I am afraid,' said he, 'one hundred pounds is too much for the Trustees to pay openly for only four leaves; still, they ought to have it at that price if necessary, or even more.' 'Now, Mr Stevens,' said Mr Panizzi, 'can you

you help us to the book without any injustice to Mr Lenox?' I replied, 'Yes, I can do it in this way. The library possesses an imperfect duplicate, "Hariot's History of Virginia," in folio, 1590, wanting the last three leaves. I have those leaves, and am able therefore to make the book perfect. I offer you then to go or send to Paris and bid for this "Dati Columbus" in Mr Libri's sale at the end of July or early in August, to the extent of £100 (subsequently raised to £120), and if I purchase it at any sum within this limit, I will give it to the British Museum in exchange for the Hariot in the condition it is now in.' They both said that this was fair and liberal, and Mr Panizzi added, 'Now let us keep our own counsel and say nothing to anybody. I will at once reduce the proposition to writing and lay it before the Trustees at their next meeting, and if they approve, it is a bargain.'

The following extract of a long letter

letter to my father in Vermont, dated London, July 3 1847, continues the story as it was written at the time: —'I expect to go to the Continent again this month. The Trustees of the British Museum meet to-day. There is before them a proposition for purchasing a rare little book to be sold soon by auction in Paris. The Museum is very desirous of having it, but they wish to avoid the notoriety of paying an extravagant price for it. It is a little Italian poem by Dati, giving an account of Columbus's first voyage. It is a tract of only four leaves, and was printed at Florence in 1493. Well, I have proposed to the librarian, Mr Panizzi, to go to Paris myself and bid for the book in my own name, to the extent, if necessary, of £100 or $500, and if I get it for that amount or under, I am to give it to the Museum in exchange for Hariot's account of Virginia, printed in English for Theodore De Bry, Frankfort 1590,

a

a book of the greatest rarity, the first English account of Virginia.'

The Trustees 'approved,' and at the end of July, instead of going over to Paris myself, I entrusted all my commissions to Messrs Payne and Foss, with a limit on the 'Dati' of £120. On the 9th of August Mr Foss handed me the book and his bill, with the remark, 'I have no doubt your friend Mr Lenox will be pleased with his bargain and his unique Italian Columbus.' The bill was for No. '1253 Lettera di Colomb. fr. 1700. Frais de la Vente, 10 per cent. 170. Fr 1870, à $^{25}/_{50}$ £73 6*s* 8*d*.' The same day, taking the precious little waif to the British Museum, I handed it to Mr Panizzi, and there was far more rejoicing over it than over the ninety and nine larger books that were rapidly coming into the Museum under the then new £10,000 annual parliamentary grant.

In the presence of Mr Winter Jones and Mr Watts, Mr Panizzi at at once delivered into my hands the duplicate Hariot, for which I gave him this acknowledgment:—'British Museum, August 9 1847. Received this day of Mr Panizzi a copy of Hariot's Virginia in English, printed at Frankfort, by Wechel, at the cost of Theodore De Bry in 1590, in exchange for Dati, La Lettera, etc., Columbus's letter in Italian, entitled La Lettera di Colomb and printed at Florence 1493, said book being No. 1253 of Libri's sale at Paris, in July-August 1847. Henry Stevens.'

Thus I won that brush for Mr Lenox, and thus Mr Lenox missed securing the Dati, a loss he ever mourned, though he fully approved of the negotiations with Mr Panizzi. That Dati was then, and still is believed to be, unique, though another copy was said to be in the Trivulzio Library in Milan. Immediately on returning to Morley's with Hariot under my arm, I added my three end leaves to complete the volume, and alone

alone in my own mind and room, there was yet more rejoicing over the acquisition of this prince of American rarities, and its fortunate completion, than over the ninety and nine other rare books I had already procured for Mr Lenox. He willingly paid me one hundred guineas for the volume when I sent it to him with a history of its capture. The whole transactions from beginning to end were, it seemed to me, a good illustration of Adam Smith's idea of free trade—a good bargain for all parties engaged in it.

X

Further Exchanges with the British Museum

OUT of this transaction as a precedent grew another, in which both Mr Lenox and Mr Panizzi were again victorious, each having made the best bargain in his own estimation. A few weeks after winning the Hariot I went for a month's tour through France and Germany, and in November 1847, went to America, all the time in active correspondence with Mr Brown and Mr Lenox, but often through my good old friend, Mr Obadiah Rich, the bibliographer. Mr Rich had in contemplation a reprint

print of Hakluyt's 'Divers Voyages' 1582, 4to, but his own copy was very imperfect. He knew of my transactions with Mr Panizzi about the Dati-Hariot exchange, and during my absence called on Mr Panizzi on my affairs, and incidentally proposed an exchange of some rare book for the Museum duplicate Hakluyt. Mr Panizzi told him that his attention had lately been called to No. 5731 of Bohn's Guinea Catalogue of 1841, 'Ames's Typographical Antiquities, or an Historical Account of the Origin and Progress of Printing in Great Britain and Ireland, containing memoirs of our Antient Printers, and a Register of Books printed by them from 1471 to 1600; considerably augmented by William Herbert, 3 vols, 1785-1790, on large paper, interleaved and bound in 6 royal quarto volumes, containing a vast quantity of Manuscript Additions and corrections by Herbert himself, prepared for a new edition,

edition, neat in russia, uncut, £15 15*s*. A portion only of the first volume of this collection has been used by Dr Dibdin in his new edition. The remainder has not been used by any bibliographer.'

On enquiry of Mr Bohn, some six or seven years after the issue of his catalogue, Mr Panizzi was told that the work had just before been ordered from New York through Mr Rich. On applying to Mr Rich Mr Panizzi received this note:—'12 Red Lion Square, October 4th [1848].—Mr Rich presents his respects to Mr Panizzi, and begs leave to inform him that he sent *Herbert's own copy of his edition of Ames, with additions* to New York; but believes that the person to whom he sent it [Mr Lenox] would have no objection to part with it, particularly in exchange for some of the Museum duplicates; and Mr Rich would engage at once to give it for the copy of Hakluyt's 'Divers Voyages,' 4to, 1582,

1582, notwithstanding that the Museum duplicate wants the two maps."

Mr Panizzi was agreeable to this proposal, but Mr Lenox was not. Having lost this work of Hakluyt in my first invoice at ten guineas by a blunder of his own, as already mentioned, and the Herbert with commission, Customs duty and expenses having cost him about £20, he was not disposed to sanction Mr Rich's proposal, but was willing to give the Herbert for another little Museum duplicate of which I had written him, viz. 'Hernando de Souto [or Soto], Relaçam verdadeira de la Florida,' Evora, en Casa de Andree Burgos, 1557, small 8vo, the original edition in Portuguese. Mr Panizzi jumped at Mr Lenox's offer (there being another fine copy in the Grenville Library under SOUTO), and laid it before the Trustees for approval. The exchange was completed in March 1849; but I believe that the Trustees at that time put a stopper

stopper on any further exchanges of duplicates.

Mr Lenox was so well pleased with his bargain that it went far to reconcile him to the loss of the Italian Columbus by Dati, which by the way he had never positively ordered, and could have had no just claim upon me for it. Herbert's Ames, the Great National work of English bibliography, thus found its way back from America into the National Library, the last enterprise of its kind which Mr Panizzi was permitted to effect, where its existence is now silently recorded in the newly printed catalogue under AMES (Joseph) as 'Another copy,' with the press mark, 824. k. 31, but placed in the Keeper's room, shelved behind the door, where it has quietly remained some thirty-five years, a mine of pure English bibliography undefiled, 'lost upon earth,' still almost if not quite unknown to outsiders, and altogether forgotten or seldom if ever consulted by insiders. One of these days however I have little doubt some prowling bibliographer will ' discover ' it, and perhaps quarrel with a brother mouser about who was first in the discovery, as two of them did in 1875 respecting Poe's unique pamphlet entitled ' Tamerlane and other Poems. By a Bostonian. Boston, 1827,' 12mo, which I bought of Mr Samuel G. Drake as one of that poet's pieces, in Boston in 1859. It was sent into the Museum in 1860 with many other Boston tracts, and was paid for in 1867 one shilling!

XI

XI

The Columbus Letters and the Vermonter's views as to the editio princeps

BOTH Mr Brown and Mr Lenox, my two chief correspondents in early days, were exceedingly sweet on everything relating to Columbus, and sometimes I found it very difficult to prevent their colliding. Mr Brown had the start, and secured the first choice in 1845 and 1846. Notably among the four editions of 1493 at seven to ten guineas each, he secured the unique Paris edition with the colophon line, not in the (Rawlinson) Bodleian or Göttingen examples of that

that edition. But in the first Libri sale in London at Sotheby's, February 19 1849, there occurred a copy of the small octavo Latin edition of the Columbus Letter in eight leaves, with two leaves for the cover on the same paper, in all ten leaves, with seven different woodcuts.

Mr Brown ordered this lot with a limit of 25 guineas, and Mr Lenox of £25. Now as my chief correspondents had been indulged with a good deal of liberty, scarcely ever considering their orders completely executed till they had received the books and decided whether or not they would keep them, I grew into the habit of considering all purchases my own until accepted and paid for. Consequently when positive orders were given, which was very seldom, I grew likewise into the habit of buying the lot as cheaply as possible, and then awarding it to the correspondent who gave the highest limit. This is not always quite fair to the owner, but in my case it would have been unfair to myself to make my clients compete, as not unfrequently the awarded lot was declined and had to go to another.

Well, in the case of this Columbus Letter, though I had five or six orders, I purchased it for £16 10*s*, and accordingly, as had been done many times before within the last five or six years without a grumble, I awarded it to the highest limit, and sent the little book to Mr John Carter Brown. Hitherto in cases of importance, Mr Lenox had generally been successful, because he usually gave the highest limit. But in this case he rebelled. He wrote that the book had gone under his commission of £25, that he knew nobody else in the transaction, and that he insisted on having it, or he should at once transfer his orders to some one else. I endeavoured to vindicate my conduct by stating our long-continued practice, with which he he was perfectly well acquainted, but without success. He grew more and more peremptory, insisting on having the book solely on the ground that it went under his limit.

At length after some months of negotiation Mr Brown, on being made acquainted with the whole correspondence, very kindly, to relieve me of the dilemma, sent the book to Mr Lenox without a word of comment or explanation, except that though it went also below his higher limit, he yielded it to Mr Lenox for peace. Mr Brown was exceedingly vexed with Mr Lenox, and pronounced the demand selfish, and under all the circumstances both illiberal and unbusinesslike. They were both old bachelors, and I suppose found it unpleasant to be crossed; while I found it sometimes difficult to navigate between them without giving offence to one or the other.

However, from that time I resorted, in cases of duplicate orders from them, to to the expedient of always putting the lot in at one bid above the lower limit, which after all, I believe, is the fairer way in the case of positive orders. This sometimes cost one of them a good deal more money, but it abated the chafing and generally gave satisfaction. Both thought the old method the fairest when they got the prize. But I was obliged on the new system of bidding to insist on the purchaser keeping the book without the option of returning it. A case in point occurred shortly after at Messrs Puttick and Simpson's, when the German Columbus Letter of 1497 occurred for sale. This time the limits were reversed, Mr Lenox's being 25 guineas and Mr Brown's £25. I bought the lot for Mr Lenox at one bidding of £26, and shortly after secured another copy for Mr Brown for less than half that price.

These specimens however were of small account, the ordered books always being but a very small percentage

tage of the rarities collected and sent out on approval. But to this little octavo Columbus hangs a bibliographical tale which may perhaps as well be noticed here as anywhere, especially as I have kept my discovery a dozen years, and the revelation of it now may possibly aid in clearing up the entangled question of the *editio princeps* of this most important publication respecting the discovery of the New World.

Mr Lenox greatly rejoiced in the acquisition of this octavo Columbus Letter, placing it as the FIRST EDITION in his bibliography of the Letter subjoined to his translation of 'Nicolaus Syllacius de Insulis Meridiani atque Indici Maris Nuper Inventis,' privately printed at New York in 1860, in quarto, Appendix p. xxxv. It is well known to the cognoscenti, that the numerous writers on the voyages of Columbus and the discovery of America are by no means agreed as to which of the many editions in Latin of of the first letter of Columbus, on his return from his first voyage in March 1493, is the original or *editio princeps.* It is a question of no little importance, as evidenced by the warm discussions of Bossi, Morelli, Navarrette, Humboldt, Brunet, Major, Lenox, Harrisse, Varnhagen, Gayangos, and others. My own forty years' bibliographical studies have led me to differ from the reasonings and conclusions of all these writers.

It was the discovery of the origin of this little octavo edition that has I think become the key to the mystery. In 1873, while at Basle, I visited the public library, and was informed by the accomplished librarian, who is well up in the history of Basle printing and printers, among other important bibliographical matters, that the celebrated printer Froben, who began printing at Basle in 1491, bequeathed his very nearly complete collection of the books printed by himself, well and carefully bound, to the

the library of a monastery over the river opposite the town, and that this extremely valuable collection had recently been transferred to the Public Library of Basle. I then, by a sort of inspiration, inquired if there was any connection between Bergman de Olpe and Froben, when it appeared that Olpe was at first a bookseller or publisher, and that some if not all of his early books of 1491-94 were printed for him by Froben, including the quarto Verardus-Columbus. In running out this idea, I was rejoiced to find among the Froben books a thick, dumpy volume of tracts in small octavo, among which was a fine and clean copy of this Libri-Stevens-Brown-Lenox octavo Columbus letter, without the two leaves of cover (the first and tenth), but with the identical woodcuts that are found in the quarto Olpe of 1494. Thus both the octavo and quarto editions were proved beyond a doubt to have come from the press of Froben.

Now

Now this important point being established, no one will I suppose for a moment contend that Froben at Basle had the honour of thus issuing the *editio princeps* in April or May 1493, but rather received a copy of the original impression from Rome in eleven or twelve days (the then usual time of transit) after publication, say about the middle of May. We know that another edition was issued in Paris by Guio Marchant in two forms, exactly alike, except that one has a colophon line and the other is without it. Besides these reprints in Latin there were two editions of Dati's translation into Italian published at Florence, October 25th and 26th 1493, all following one and the same prototype, probably the 34-line, Gothic letter edition without date, name of printer or place, but generally attributed to the press of Stephen Planck of Rome, at the end of April or beginning of May 1493, when Pope Alexander's 'demarcation'

tion' bull of the 4th of May was printed and published. All these reprints alike follow certain characteristics that are unmistakable.

The announcement of so great a discovery would spread like wild-fire throughout Christendom, and hence the prompt reprints of Basle and Paris, and the poetic translation of Florence. Is it at all likely that these reprinters would delay a day for a new and revised edition? Certainly not. *Ergo*, I think that both the Basle and the Paris editions, as well as the work of Dati, followed the original announcement. Now from certain points in the title (which was added by the translator into Latin), and certain specimens of bad grammar or typographical errors or false readings, etc., which appear alike in all these reprints, it is not difficult in my judgment to trace the parent edition. The Latin of the first edition is crude and puerile, and hence probably the much changed edition

 of

of Eucharius Silber, Rome 1493, and the one of 33 lines with similar readings, generally attributed to the press of Stephen Planck, without date or names of place and printer, are both subsequent to the original issue.

This original, as well as the Basle and Paris reprints, all have the name of Ferdinand only in the title, with Aliander of Cosco as the translator the 29th of April 1493, while the two other Rome editions have Ferdinand and Isabella with Leander. It is very likely that a young gentleman of extraordinary precocity in languages, named Aliander, then attached to the Vatican Library, and subsequently a sort of Mezzofanti, was the puerile translator for the Pope. These facts and suggestions, submitted to Mr Lenox in the autumn of 1873, shook his faith in his octavo *editio princeps*. These points interested him very much, and will be worked out more fully in another place.

Mr

Mr Lenox was a great stickler for naked truth, and seldom expressed positive opinions except when he had formed them. When therefore he had booked an opinion he was very tenacious of it, though he might have forgotten the particular process on which it was based. It was therefore sometimes a little pleasant to show him that somebody else as well as myself sometimes made mistakes or arrived at wrong conclusions. This *editio princeps* of Columbus's Letter was a case in point. He desired to possess it above all things because he then believed it to be the first edition. He was thus unconsciously led into a selfish argument that would not hold water. He subsequently abandoned that idea, though he was less positive about the original.

XII

XII

Washington's Farewell Address

ABOUT 1847 or 1848 it was announced by the administrators of the late David C. Claypoole of Philadelphia, proprietor and editor of the 'Daily Advertiser,' that they were about to sell by auction in that city the original autograph manuscript of Washington's Farewell Address, given to Claypoole by Washington himself in September 1796. Mr Lenox bought it against the Congress Library for $2,200 I think, while some blamed him for competing against the Government Library, where such a national relic ought to

find

find a resting-place. He however offered the library committee not to compete under their limit, if they would tell him how far they intended to go. They declined to tell him their limit, or even if they intended to buy it, so he very properly disregarded them. There is probably no class of appointed men so often called upon to decide without experience as library committees, whose chief delight seems to be to sit on librarians disposed to independent decisions.

Mr Lenox all his life was his own library committee. In 1850 he privately printed this precious manuscript with variorum notes and other illustrative papers in one of thc most sumptuous volumes ever issued in the United States up to that time, '54 copies folio, 175 copies quarto. Printed for Presents only.' He had most of the copies expensively and appropriately bound in morocco extra, with emblematic toolings in gold. On coming to Europe in May 1852,

1852, he brought several copies with him for distribution among libraries and friends. In June he brought to my office at Morley's about a dozen copies inscribed to libraries and individuals, with a view of my having them done up, addressed and distributed free of cost to the recipients. On looking over the copy inscribed to me, I complimented him on the beauty, taste and finish of the volume. 'Yes,' said he, 'until I undertook to print that work, I never knew the difficulty of printing without typographical errors. The whole book was read over many, many times, both by myself and several literary friends, but never without discovering some provoking blunder. But we persevered, having it all in type, until after a dozen or more revises, no one of us could find another misprint, and so I then gave orders for it to go to press. It is said that the Oxford University Press offers a guinea for every typographical error in in its Bibles. I should not fear to make a similar offer respecting this book, for I am thoroughly convinced that the printing is absolutely correct.'

'Yes, Mr Lenox,' I replied, 'the book at sight appears perfect. The leaves as you turn them over seem to talk to you, but this one I am now looking at appears to grumble, I suppose, because of the words "three drafts of such a papar." Why "papar" instead of "paper"?' He cast his quick eye on the page. It was even so. His 'pride of accuracy' evaporated in a moment, and he wilted into my arm-chair as if he had been shot. It was I believe his first book, and he was ill prepared for such a calamity. I pitied his distress. 'Well,' at last he said, 'it is my own fault, "and pity 'tis, 'tis true." What in the world am I to do? I much dislike an erratum note, and it is a great deal of trouble to cancel the leaf and rebind the volume. I am distressed beyond measure.' 'Never mind,' said I, 'we'll fix

fix it. Leave the books with me, and come here to-morrow at this hour. In all these copies the error shall be made to disappear.' 'I am,' said he, 'so helpless and reckless now, that I shall do as you say, for I can never present the copies with the knowledge that they contain such a blunder.'

He went away despondent, and I immediately sent to my old friend, John Harris senior, to come with his tools to my office at once for a few hours' work. On examining the stout, well-sized paper, Harris immediately comprehended the remedy, and placing a thick *lignum vitæ* round ruler under the word 'papar,' with a keen razor carefully shaved off the ink from the letter 'a' without hardly touching the fibre underneath. Having done the same to all the copies, he next with a fine camel-hair pencil replaced it with an 'e' with ink coloured to match the surrounding letters, in an inimitable manner, as John Harris alone could do it. When Mr

Mr Lenox called the next day the old artist was there to show him his handywork. The restoration was perfect, and not to be detected by Mr Lenox, who was if possible more delighted than he was despondent the day before. After thanking Harris, he inquired how much he was to be paid. 'Well,' said Harris, 'since you appear to be so well pleased with my work, and I have had to do it here, I shall venture to ask you fifteen shillings for the twelve copies.' 'And cheap enough too,' replied Mr Lenox, handing him a sovereign; 'and pray take this too, besides my best thanks, as a mark of my appreciation,' handing him another sovereign. My own copy of the book was not so corrected, I preferring to keep it as a memorial of the fallibility of one of the most exact and conscientious men I ever knew. See Preface, page iv line 9.

XIII

The Collection of Hulsius. The Wycliffe manuscripts. Washington's Library

BUT 'Finis' beckons, while there is room left to only summarize a few of the many remaining jottings of my reminiscences of Mr Lenox. Perhaps some of these dropt stitches may be picked up in another place. I intended to speak of our luck, perseverance and hairbreadth escapes, in bringing together his extraordinary collections of De Bry, Hulsius, Thevenot, Haertgerts, Saeghman, Colyn, Hakluyt, Purchas, etc. The newspaper stories of the extent and cost

of

of the Lenox De Bry are wild and bottomless, yet it is one of the best and most comprehensive sets known. His Hulsius it is believed was without a rival at the time of his death. In 1847 I provided him with a complete set, mixed editions, of the 27 parts (counting part eleven as two) for £25! after having supplied the Ternaux-Compans set to Mr Brown at the same price. Then commenced his more than thirty years' struggle for all the other editions, cancels, variations, etc., which resulted in his marvellous set. At everything known he aimed, and acquired much hitherto unknown, but he was finally obliged to submit to the humiliation of knowing of three important variations which he never could win, and was therefore forced to supply them in facsimile. All these editions and variations, picked up separately from many sources, cost him much research over a long time, besides many hundreds of pounds. Since his death in 1880,

my

my long watchfulness in his behalf has been rewarded by finding, at considerable cost, all these three *desiderata*. But they came into my net, alas! too late for Mr Lenox, and therefore now go to adorn my own matchless set of Hulsius, which in the various editions extends to over sixty volumes. I meant also to have spoken of the five Caxtons and the block books to which I helped him, besides the two early manuscript New Testaments by Wycliffe, one of which in octavo, about 1410, has the long Prologue to the Romans, not included in the 4-volume Oxford edition of 1850, and though known to Sir Frederick Madden, was never seen by him until I lent him this MS., before sending it to Mr Lenox in August 1859 for £188 6*s*. It was bound by F. Bedford in brown morocco, antique pattern, and protected in a suitable morocco pull-off case, and is still one of the pearls of the Lenox Library.

I have left no room to speak of the extraordinary American collection of Mr Ternaux-Compans, he of the Merino-sheep's head, bought at a bargain by Mr Rich in 1844, and mostly distributed by me in 1845 to Mr Carter Brown and Mr Lenox, and a few other clients, at prices that were then fairly remunerative, but which now seem ridiculously low. In 1848 I bought Washington's Library of about 3,000 volumes, for $3,000, to secure about 300 volumes with the autograph of the 'Father of his country' on the title-pages, some rarities for Mr Lenox, and many tracts and miscellaneous American books for the British Museum. Mr Lenox declined the books with autographs, and there being a great hue and cry raised in Boston against my sending them out of the country, I sold the collection to a parcel of Bostonians for $5,000, but after passing that old Boston hat round for two or three months for $50 subscriptions,

scriptions, only $3,250 could be raised, and therefore, as I had used a few hundred dollars of the money advanced to me by the promoters and was in a tight place, I was compelled to subscribe the rest myself to make up the amount of the purchase. I reserved to myself five volumes with choice autographs, two of which were sold to Mr Lenox, one for £20 and the other for £50, the remaining three being presented to the British Museum, the Bodleian, and the Royal Library of Berlin.

XIV

XIV

The Aspinwall, Drake, Crowninshield and Humboldt Libraries. Tyndale's Pentateuch. The Juan de la Cosa Map

YEAR or two later, while in treaty for the whole of the Aspinwall Library for Mr Brown, Mr Lenox, Dr Cogswell, and for the British Museum, I catalogued the whole collection, putting an agreed price on every book, satisfactory to Colonel Aspinwall and myself. But on summing up the total it came to a little over £1,200, some £800 less than he expected; so the Colonel flew off the bargain and I escaped a lot of foolishness.

ishness. Mr Lenox and Mr.Brown thought my prices for the rarities they wanted too high, and one of Dr Cogswell's library committee finding one of his own tracts priced at half-a-crown, said, what was perhaps quite true, that the work was over-priced; that he would present a copy to the library, but he wanted nothing more to do with the Aspinwall Collection or Mr Stevens's prices. Thus this wiseacre on the committee of trustees of the Astor Library sat on Dr Cogswell, and rendered him powerless to complete any part of the purchase. ''Twas ever thus,' wrote Dr Cogswell, 'one committee-man, stiff in his ignorance, may thwart the best schemes of an intelligent librarian who understands his business and comprehends the wants of the community.'

In 1858 I bought Mr S. G. Drake's library, and in 1859 Mr E. A. Crowninshield's, each for $10,000, having in my eye in both cases certain

tain choice 'Historical Nuggets' for Mr Lenox, who was ever ready to pay good prices for an early choice. In 1860 I paid £4,000 for the Humboldt Library, but the war coming on after I had got the immense bulk in London, I was crushed by the weight of it. Dr Cogswell had encouraged me to the venture, by giving me to understand that the trustees of the Astor Library would select at once between £2,000 and £3,000 worth, and Mr Lenox had intimated that he should be glad to secure as usual certain of the rarities. On the first gun of Fort Sumter all these and many other clients shut up like clam shells, and began to practise those beautiful virtues of prudence and economy which protected themselves and at the same time ruined me.

I ought to have mentioned the well-known sales of Libri, Payne & Foss, Pickering, Lord Stewart de Rothesay, Dr Hawtry, Dun Gardner, Offor,

 and

and many others, at which I bought largely for Mr Lenox. At one of these sales Mr Lenox sent an order for Tyndale's Pentateuch 1530, with a limit of £50, or more if I thought it desirable after inspection. I had to pay £159 for it, which with commission and expenses, cost Mr Lenox £175. The day after the sale Lord Ashburnham offered me 200 guineas for the volume, but it was Mr Lenox's. The volume was bound in morocco with heavy boards, and cost the purchaser more than three times its weight in sovereigns. The book had three interior leaves in facsimile by the elder Harris, which in my humble judgment very much depreciated its value, though otherwise the largest, purest and finest copy known. Subsequently, at infinite pains, I had another copy through my hands, and arranged to supply the originals of these three leaves for £20, and sent them by post to Mr Lenox for the purpose of completing his

his volume. But he was not of my way of thinking. The three leaves were three-eighths of an inch shorter than his, and therefore as they would not grow, he returned them to me! That same copy, with those same three leaves, would now produce probably not less than 500 guineas. A similar copy, wanting the whole of the Book of Genesis with the date, was sold by auction at Sotheby's in 1884 for £200, and is now one of the chiefest ornaments of the Astor Library.

In May 1853 the Walckenaer sale took place in Paris. I ordered many books from it for Mr Brown and Mr Lenox on my own responsibility, they not having received the catalogue in time. In this sale No 2904 was the large manuscript map of the wor'd by Juan de la Cosa, executed at Santa Maria in Spain in the year 1500, rendered famous by Humboldt, altogether then and even now the most precious cartographical document

document relating to the New World. Mr Brown turned up in London just as I was ordering it, but had no appreciative fancy for it. So I determined to go it alone, and sent my intelligent and reliable agent in Paris a limit of 1,000 francs for it. He replied confidentially that he was aware of an order in town from a great foreign public library with a limit considerably exceeding mine, which I took to be the British Museum. Wishing very much to secure the prize, I at once replied requesting him to double my limit. The next post brought me another letter that 2,000 francs was not yet enough, for he was assured that M. Jomard, of the Royal Library, would outbid me. As time was getting short, and my anxiety to win was increasing, I wrote him the evening before the sale to again double my limit, if that in his judgment was not sheer folly. So I left my limit to him anywhere under 4,000 francs. The Queen of Spain won the chase at 4,020 francs and

and I had the honour of coming in the loser by a neck, but with nothing to pay; and so also Mr Lenox escaped. The Naval Museum at Madrid (Catalogue No. 553) is said now to hold this precious geographical document, worth cartloads of the Portuguese Cantino map lately brought to light, with its duplicate Cuba and purely bogus and conjectural geography, based on Portuguese misreadings and misunderstandings of the exaggerated geographical accounts of the first and second voyages of Columbus.

XV

The Vermonter dabbleth in Nineveh Marbles

IN 1858 Mr Lenox, at an expense of $3,000, presented to the New York Historical Society a large collection of Nineveh sculptures, which the Council of the Society, in gratitude for the highly valued collection, voted should be named and thenceforward be known and styled the 'Lenox Marbles.' My notes and reminiscences of that collection may perhaps be recorded here. After Mr Layard and Colonel Rawlinson had completed their researches, and shipped their selected discoveries to the British Museum,

Museum, many duplicates were reburied to preserve them from the natives. Mr Williams the American missionary, made great efforts to have these valuable duplicates secured for America, and wrote to Mr Abbot Lawrence, the United States Minister in London. This correspondence I caused to be laid before the Trustees of the Museum, who promptly replied that early in 1852 they had instructed Colonel Rawlinson to facilitate others in removing such sculptures as were not required for the British Museum. Mr Lawrence's application to the Smithsonian Institution through me, and to the authorities of Washington direct, were permitted to slumber in the mighty limbo there of such expensive ventures, and nothing was done.

Meanwhile two English merchants, one a consul, residing at Bagdad or Mosul, who had been friends of Layard and Rawlinson during their excavations, obtained permission to remove

remove thirteen large slabs, and in 1852 floated them 800 miles down the Tigris to the Persian Gulf, and thence shipped them to the Mauritius, and thence trans-shipped them to London, where they lay stored in the East India Docks many months, like many other speculative adventures, eating their heads off. Some changes having occurred in the plans or prospects of the proprietors, their London agent came to me with a note of introduction from Barings, with a view of transferring their hungry charge to the Smithsonian Institution or to Uncle Samuel. But neither Professor Henry nor my Uncle made any sign or sent any ship for them. Finally, a little later, when the news of the unfortunate loss of the vessel containing the entire excavations of the French reached this country, I at once, after consulting my friends Dr Birch and Mr Vaux of the British Museum as to their genuineness and archæological value, determined to purchase the

the whole collection on my own account. They were offered to me, if I would pay all the bills of charges on them from Mosul to the East India Docks, including the dock charges and storage, in all amounting to only £300, receiving them then and there accoutred as they were. In October 1853 I shipped the whole in their original bulky log fastenings by the good ship 'Nabob' direct to Boston, consigning them, with insurance and freight paid to destination, to Messrs Hubbard Brothers.

With head full of Layard's books, I had golden dreams about these Nineveh sculptures, 3,000 years old, landing at Boston only 245 years after John Winthrop; and about their reception at the Hub of the universe. The first reality I experienced when fully awake was that the expenses were running up very fast, and that I was compelled to disregard the 'ancient art' and pay for the sculptured marbles, in their bulky protections, as goods of 30 tons measurement, though the actual weight was only about 17 tons. They consisted of 13 slabs, about a foot thick, with sculptures in bas-relief, generally about 7½ feet high, and averaging 6 feet in width, the whole, ranged side by side, measuring 72 feet 2 inches. I wrote fully to Mr Edward Everett, Mr George Sumner, Mr George Livermore and others about the consignment, and at the request of Mr Joshua Bates I wrote out a full statement, with vouchers from men in the British Museum as to their value and genuine character, which documents Mr Bates sent to Mr George Ticknor, President of the Trustees of the Free Public Library.

At first all wrote encouragingly, and the 'ancients' were favourably greeted on their being landed and stored on Long Wharf. Eventually, after some months, with fresh expenses for storage, the public-spirited citizens

citizens had them removed to the Boston Athenæum at their own cost, and set up for profitable exhibition. Here they stood many more weary months, like Barnum's wax figures, until they and I were tired.

Finally in 1858, when I was in New York, I related the history of my patriotic adventure in the Nineveh fine arts line, to my old and valued friend Mr George H. Moore, of the New York Historical Society. He at once appreciated the situation in all its bearings, and with an enthusiasm akin to that of the Green Mountain Boy who captured them in the East India Docks, said, 'By thunder, Henry, wouldn't it be a mighty fine thing to transfer them to the ground floor room in our Historical Society! What'll you take for the lot, delivered free on the railway trucks in Boston?' 'Do you mean it, George?' 'Yes, honour bright.' 'Well,' said I, 'they have cost me during the last five years well

well nigh $3,000, and though earning nothing now, they are costing me nothing where they are, excepting the interest on the outlay. You may now have them, as I had them, by paying the bills. The Athenæum has had two annual exhibitions out of them, and as they stand there subject to my order, I should have no hesitation in ordering them away at once in case the Bostonians are not disposed to complete the purchase without further delay.'

George was in earnest, and I sent a confidential friend, well posted in such matters, to inquire into the facts, and ascertain if the authorities were disposed to buy the lot. If so, they of course had the pre-emption, otherwise the 'goods' would be speedily removed to be sold elsewhere. The report was that there was little inclination in the parties interested in Boston to purchase, and 'that Mr Stevens of course could remove his "Nineveh Marbles" whenever he pleased,

pleased, and he would be entitled to our thanks for lending them to us for so long a time.' All appeared perfectly fair, serene and friendly; but one high-minded Beacon Streeter, a little more frank than the others, obligingly communicated to my friend, not knowing that he was also my agent, the important fact 'that it was wholly unnecessary for us to buy those ponderous sculptures, for they will cost Mr Stevens as much as they are worth to remove them to another town.' On further inquiry he found that this Fabian policy of masterly inactivity pervaded all the interested brain-carriers of the modern Athens.

After conning over this intelligence and report together, George said, 'Well, Henry, this is Boston all over, and another piece of your Washington Autograph-Book business a few years ago. If you wish the thing to go through you will have to subscribe for the lion's share of of the stock yourself. "Three thousand ducats—'tis a good round sum," but we'll remove our neighbour's Nineveh marble landmarks to New York. Come and see me to-morrow, after I have seen Mr Lenox and told him the story.' The next day when we met George said, 'Well Henry, it is o.k.; let us go on to Boston and see those Sennacherib men with their stone carpet-bags. Mr Lenox says that if I find all things correct he will give us a cheque for $3,000 as soon as the goods reach New York to my satisfaction.' So the business was accomplished in a few days, and so the 'Stevens marbles' became the 'Lenox marbles,' and at last found a permanent resting-place; and thus it was that I recouped my money, and exercised my patience in performing another patriotic deed for a naughty New World. The next time I saw Mr Lenox I congratulated him on his successful play at marbles, and hoped he would be luckier than

I

I had been with those men and memorials of old. He replied that the venture formed a part of his 'Bible Collection,' but the Historical Society had to pasture them.

XVI

XVI

Cromwell's Letter to John Cotton. G. M.B.'s first interview with Mr Lenox. The Coverdale Map of 1574. *The* 1611 *unique Testament in* 12°. *'La Carta universale delle terra firme' of* 1534

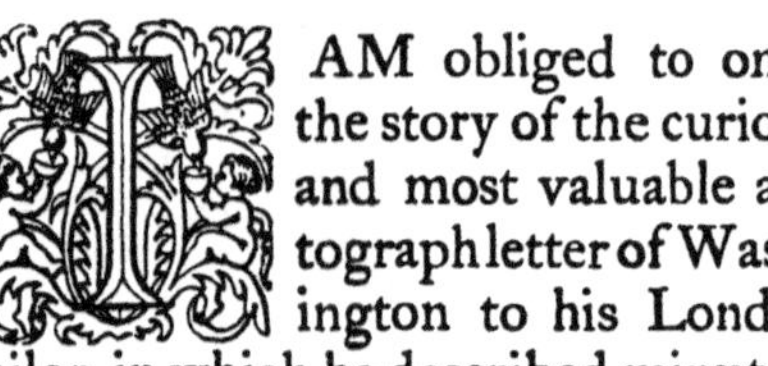

AM obliged to omit the story of the curious and most valuable autograph letter of Washington to his London tailor, in which he described minutely the dimensions and proportions of his figure, even to the number of inches in his waist, the length of his legs and arms, as well as the circumference of his chest, knees and thighs; which letter I procured and sent to Mr Lenox in in April 1852 for the very moderate sum of three guineas. What would it bring now? Nor is there room to just more than mention the particulars of a long autograph letter of Oliver Cromwell to John Cotton of Boston in N.E., dated October 2d 1651, which I procured and induced him to purchase for £40 in February 1854. Oliver addressed his letter 'For my esteemed freind, Mr Cotton, Pastor to the church att Boston in New England, theise,' and begins 'Worthye Sr. and my Christian freind, I received yours a few dayes sithence, it was welcom to mee, because signed by you, whome I loue and Honour in the Lord but more to see some of the same grounds of our Actinges Stirringe in you, that haue in vs, to qviet vs to our worke, and support vs therein, wch hath had greatest difficultye in our engagement in Scotland, by reason wee haue had to doe wth some, whoe were (I verily thinke) Godly, but thorough weakenesse, and the subtiltye of Sathan inuolved in interests against the Lord, and his people ... [*ending*] I tooke this libertye from businesse to salute you thus in a word, trulye I am ready to serue you and the rest of our brethren, and the churches wth you. I am a poore weake creature, not worthye the name of a worme, yett accepted to serve the Lord and his people, indeed my deare freind betweene you and mee you knowe not mee, my weaknessees, my inordinate passions, my vngratefullnesse, and euery way vnfitness to my worke, yett, yett the Lord whoe will haue mercye on whom He will, does as you see. Pray for mee, salute all Christian freinds though vnknown, I rest Your affectionate freind to serve you O. CROMWELL.' Mr Lenox printed this letter as No. 4 of his 'Curiosities of "American" Literature.'

A paragraph might be made respecting our first interview in New York

York in the late autumn of 1847, when we saw each other for the first time after more than two years of active correspondence, and when by comparing notes, we were both very much mistaken in the portraits our fancies had painted of each other. On arriving at the Astor House I dropped Mr Lenox a line to say I was in town, and would be glad to see him at any time and place most convenient to himself. By return of boy, the answer came, 'To-morrow morning at nine o'clock at my house.' During the day all my gossiping and bookish friends greeted me cordially, and said, 'Now we shall hear and know something of Mr Lenox, his library and new house.'

The next morning, on the stroke of nine, I mounted the broad stone steps and rang the bell. A maiden servant opened the door on the chain six or eight inches, and asked, 'Are you Mr Stevens?' 'Yes.' 'Mr Lenox is in his office below; you can enter

enter by the door under the steps.' Down I went and again rang a bell, when Mr Lenox himself unlocked a door and an iron gate and gave me a warm welcome. We talked and rambled about for four hours and made each other's personal acquaintance pretty fast, while I saw him, his library, gallery and a room or two besides the hall, and many closed doors. My impression of him was altogether favourable, but by his manner, more than by anything he said, I came to the conclusion that the treasures of his mind, as a matter of habit, like his front door, always 'had the chain up.' He was frank, open and serene to me, but without his saying it in so many words I came to the conclusion that my future policy was to 'put up my chain' also so far as any personal gossip of and about him was concerned.

Thenceforth Mr Lenox was always allowed to have his own way, without any dictation or strong argument from

from me. He had a mind of his own and a fortune to back it. My gossiping friends the next day and often afterwards sat on me in Bartlett and Welford's store, where they used most to congregate, but they were welcome to all the interior news they extracted. I had already learned to put up my Lenox chain. Mr Lenox and I stood on a level, as far as I could see, he a buyer and I a seller; he collecting to shelve, I collecting to disperse—one's calling necessary to the other's. If there were any real difference of rank, it is not likely either of us ever saw or thought of it. We often saw each other for the next eighteen months, but never except by appointment. This mutual courtesy and equality always continued between us, though he bought while I sold.

Some years later he said to me, 'As you seem to find everything you want sooner or later, I wish you would find me a copy of the Coverdale woodcut map of the Holy Land with the

the date 1574, from the identical block with that of the 1535 Bible, having only the date and certain inscriptions altered.' 'I will try,' was my reply. Two or three weeks later, while travelling up Connecticut River, I stopped a day or two at Charlestown, New Hampshire, and calling on Mr Silvester there, I saw a very imperfect copy of the folio Bishops' Bible of 1574 with this very map, fine and perfect. By a little negotiation, after the true Yankee style, I became possessed of the volume, and took it back to Mr Lenox in triumph. 'I never!' said he; and he paid me fifty dollars for the map. I have never since been able to procure another copy.

During the war Mr Lenox suspended generally his ardent foraging for rare books, and only occasionally had an intermittent attack of his old bibliographical fever. Early in 1866, after I had sent him some extraordinary historical nuggets that he could not

not resist buying, he wrote me on Shakespeare's birth and death day, April 23, a long letter, in which was contained this announcement: 'Your best plan, as far as I am concerned, will be to let me have a memorandum beforehand of what you suppose I may take, and I will let you know immediately what you shall forward to me. In fact, unless it be some volume like the Vesputius, or De Bry, or Hulsius, or Jesuit Relation, I have *almost* made up my mind to stop purchasing.' Such hints between 1865 and 1875 I not unfrequently had from him in his numerous letters on bibliographical subjects, while sometimes an amusing commentary on these incipient resolutions was found in a postscript, in which he inquired anxiously for some nugget that he had passed or missed when under his eye, but now desired me to re-offer or procure for him.

There were some books which Mr Lenox bought with reluctance, being, he he thought, 'too dear,' but which he soon learned to appreciate and value as historical pearls of great price. Among these was the Barker, London 1611, 12° long-line, small black letter first edition of the New Testament of the 1611 version, then considered unique, as described by Lea Wilson under his No. 57, and in Pickering's auction catalogue, part 2 No. 3534, in 1854. The cost to him including my commission, was £37 *2s. 6d.*, besides freight, insurance and the Customs duty. That precious little volume, after forty years' bibliographical research by Bible students and collectors, still remains unique. Were it now to come into the market again, how it would open the eyes of bibliographers, and empty the pockets of some lucky collector! No historian has as yet told us why that pocket edition was printed by Robert Barker, the King's printer, and probably never published. Why and for what reason was it suppressed?

Another

Another book, sent him in April 1852, about which he hesitated on account of the price of eighteen guineas but afterwards held as priceless, was 'Libro primo, secondo & ultimo,' by Peter Martyr, Oviedo and Xeres, edited by Ramusio, and printed at Venice in 1534, with the usual map of 'Spagnvola,' and the large and unique map entitled 'La carta universale della terra firme.' This latter, the largest and perhaps the most important of the early woodcut maps of the New World, has to this day remained unique. Mr Panizzi tried very hard to induce me to let him have this map for the British Museum, and offered me for it my price for the book and map; but I told him that it had been reported to Mr Lenox, but if declined the Museum should have it. At Mr Panizzi's suggestion, I employed the elder John Harris to make a careful fac-simile tracing of it for me, which was thrown on to stone, and some copies published by me. See 'Nuggets,' No. 1808, and my 'Geographical Notes' for a reduced copy of it. No second copy of the original, as far as I can learn, has as yet been brought to light. The fac-simile has erroneously been quoted as Mr Harris's publication. I have several copies still on hand.

XVII

XVII

The fac-simile leaves in the quarto Hariot. The true history of the 'Hunt-Lenox Globe.' John White's Virginia Drawings. Ludd's 'Speculi Orbis Descriptio'

R LENOX was principled against raffles, wagers, lotteries and games of chance generally, but I once led him into a sort of bet in this way, by which I won from him £4. I had acquired a fair copy of that gem of rare books, the quarto edition of 'Hariot's briefe and true report of the new found land of Virginea, London, Feb. 1588,' wanting four leaves in the body of the book. These I had

had very skilfully traced by Harris, transferred to stone, printed off on old paper of a perfect match, the book and these leaves sized and coloured alike, and bound in morocco by Bedford. The volume was then sent to Mr Lenox to be examined by him *de visu*, the price to be £25; but if he could detect the four fac-simile leaves, and would point them out to me without error, the price was to be reduced to £21. By the first post after the book was received he remitted me the twenty guineas, with a list of the fac-similes. But on my informing him that two of *his* fac-similes were originals, he immediately remitted the four pounds and acknowledged his defeat.

In 1870, while residing at the 'Clarendon' in New York, I dined one evening with Mr R. M. Hunt, the architect of the Lenox Library, a son of my father's old friend Jonathan Hunt, who represented the State of Vermont in Congress from 1827

to

to 1832. While talking on library conveniences and plans, I chanced to notice a small copper globe, a child's plaything, rolling about the floor. On inquiry, I was told that he picked it up in some town in France for a song, and now, as it opened at the equator and was hollow, the children had appropriated it for their amusement. I saw at once by its outlines that it was probably older than any other globe known, except Martin Behaim's at Nurnberg, and perhaps the Leon globe, and told Mr Hunt my opinion of its geography, requesting him to take great care of it, for it would some day make a noise in the geographical world. Subsequently I borrowed it for two or three months, studied it, took it to Washington, exhibited it to Dr Hilgard and others at the Coast Survey Office, and employed one of the draughtsmen there to project it in a two-hemisphere map, with a diameter of the original, about five and a half inches,

inches, at a cost to me of $20. On returning to New York I delivered it into the hands of Mr Hunt, telling him that it was unquestionably as early as 1510 and perhaps 1505, and was in historical and geographical interest second to hardly any other globe, small as it was; and concluded by recommending him, when he and his children had done playing with it, to present it to the Lenox Library, the plans of which he was then engaged upon. I also told Mr Lenox of it and its value, and recommended him to keep his eye upon it, and secure it if possible for preservation in his library. My pains and powder were not thrown away. Not long after Mr Hunt presented it to the library, and from that time it has been known and styled as the 'Hunt-Lenox Globe.' On my return to London I showed my drawing of it to my friend Mr C. H. Coote, of the map department of the British Museum, and lent it to him for the reduced

duced fac-simile in his article on GLOBES in the new edition of the 'Encyclopædia Britannica.' Thus the 'Hunt-Lenox Globe' won its geographical niche in literature as well as in 'Narrative History.'

Notwithstanding all these rarities that Mr Lenox by his enterprise and liberality secured for his library, he sometimes missed his opportunities, and failed to shoot the folly as it rose. Among the numerous 'pearls of great price' that passed through my hands, and he permitted to slip through his fingers, may be mentioned the following:—1. Captain John White's 73 original water-colour drawings in 1585-86, while acting with Hariot in Raleigh's first expedition, representing the men, women, beasts, birds, fish, plants, etc., of Virginia, 23 of which had been engraved by De Bry in his Part I. Frankfort 1590. These drawings, showing the English origin of De Bry's famous collection, were first offered to Mr Lenox, and on being

being declined, were sold to the British Museum for £235, and by Mr Panizzi placed in the Grenville Library, where they are esteemed of inestimable artistic and historical value. Mr Lenox wrote me the 23rd April 1866:—'I think you have made a good sale of your White's drawings to the Museum. I shall be glad to see your report to the trustees on the subject. I hope you will not forget it.'

2. Walter Ludd's 'Speculi Orbis descriptio,' printed at St Dié in 1508, a small folio tract of a few leaves, expensively bound in red morocco by Bedford, a sort of key to the Vespucci books and the Cosmographiæ Introductio, was another unknown nugget which I took infinite pains to study and place in America. Mr Lenox and all my other correspondents there declined it at ten guineas. So after having offered it also to the British Museum with like success, I threw it into auction at Sotheby's, where it

was

was bought for the Museum for £8 8*s*, I having called Mr Winter Jones's particular attention to it and the explanatory note in the auction catalogue, thus costing with commission £9 4*s* 9*d*. The day after its delivery at the Museum, I called Mr Major's attention to it, and he made a good use of the little work in his forthcoming Prince Henry, which notice immediately raised my goose to a swan. On writing again to Mr Lenox respecting its progress, and regretting his oversight, he replied, 1st July 1867: 'Your "Speculi Orbis Descriptio" is of value merely as a reference to sustain the attempt to deprive Hylacomylas of his labour.' This was in a long letter respecting M. D'Avezac and the Cosmographiæ Introductio. The fact appears to have been that Mr Lenox so strongly espoused Humboldt's and D'Avezac's somewhat crude notions about Hylacomylas or Waldseemuler, that he could not abide the evidence that perhaps Philesius or Matthias Ringmann, instead of Waldseemuler, was after all the prime moving spirit among that famous geographical fraternity at St. Dié, who wrote up Vespucci at the expense of Columbus, and gave the name America to the New World. Ludd's Speculum still remains an historical gem of the first water.

XVIII

XVIII

Mr Lenox passes over several important 'Nuggets,' including the collection of 275 Mathers and Stuart's Portrait of Washington

SOME months before going to America in 1868, I had sent on inspection to Mr Lenox a score or two of very rare books which I imagined would strongly attract his attention, notwithstanding his intermittent notices of his intention to cease purchasing. To my great surprise, he selected several that I cared very little about and declined those that I, as caterer and bibliographer, was sweetest upon. Among these was

a

a little book of seven pages, beautifully bound in Pratt's best red morocco, with panelled sides and rich inside tooled borders. It was entitled 'A Declaration of former Passages and Proceedings betwixt the English and the Narrowgansets, with their Confederates, &c. Published by order of the Commissioners of the United Colonies. At Boston the 11 of the sixth month, 1645.' [Printed by Stephen Daye, Cambridge, N.E. 1645. 4°.] It was signed 'Jo: Winthrop, President. In the name of all the Commisioners.'

This little book was so rare and historically important that before parting with it I had it carefully transcribed, lest the hungry sea should swallow it, and it be lost sight of for ever. All the rejected, including this precious little nugget, priced at ten guineas or $50, together with about a hundred other rare books, big and little, all pertaining to what Mr Brown always called the 'great subject,'

subject,' were packed in a very large box and sent by my agent, with a new invoice, to Providence, for the approval and selection of Mr Brown. He was much pleased with the consignment, and selected a large part of the books; but like Mr Lenox, he passed the 'Narrowgansets,' though a Rhode Island book, alleging that the price was too dear. The box was repacked and stored away subject to my orders.

Some months after, being in Hartford one day gossiping with my old friend George Brinley about the uncertainty of book collectors' fancies, and telling him that I could never count on my correspondents' likes and dislikes; that in London I was choked up with nuggets that had been declined by all my chief customers as too dear or of not sufficient interest, and yet were, in my own judgment, every way as attractive to me as the majority of those they had selected, and I instanced as cases in point

point my unique collection of above 275 'Mathers' that had been declined by the Trustees of the British Museum, Mr Lenox and Mr Brown, and this 'Narrowganset' book. 'What,' said he, 'do you mean to say that you have a little book such as you describe, signed by John Winthrop and printed at Cambridge by Stephen Daye in 1645, that has been declined at ten guineas by both of those gentlemen after having been sent to them on inspection?' 'It is even so,' I replied; 'but I am used to it, as the smoke said to account for its going up a crooked chimney. It is no new thing with me, and I do not suppose that it argues anything more against their intelligence than it does against my foolishness. We think differently and have a right to. I sometimes deem my stock of nuggets, that has been picked over by the "council of ten," representing my clients in Europe and America, as rather purified than depleted by their selections.

selections. If I offer a hundred of my nuggets to Mr Brown, Mr Lenox or the British Museum, and one half is taken, I do not consider that the rest is depreciated in value because the consignment has been "picked over." Often the plums settling at the bottom are left.'

'Well,' he asked, 'may I have the Narrowgansets at the same price?' 'Yes.' 'Then I'll have it; but now comes the rub. How can we get at it without arousing Mr Brown's or Mr Bartlett's attention? If it is inquired for separately, especially for me, and they see it again, they will be sure to keep it.' It was then arranged that the 'Express' should call on Mr Brown in Providence, and without naming its destination, should bring the big box with its entire contents, at Mr Brinley's expense, overland to Hartford. In this manner Mr Brinley scored a double, and was bibliographically happy. After his death, eight or nine years later, this little book

book, fully described by Dr Trumbull under lot 754, was sold by auction in New York, in the Brinley sale part I, in March 1878, for $218, considerably more than four times my price. That goose is now a swan.

The larger portion of my 'Mather Collection' above alluded to had already found a resting-place in Mr Brinley's library. It was the result of many years of active book-hunting. The books were generally in excellent order, and were mostly bound by Bedford and Pratt in their best style in morocco or calf. After the collection had been offered and declined by both Mr Lenox and Mr Brown, it was offered entire (barring the duplicates) to the British Museum about 1862 at the same prices. Mr W. B. Rye, during Mr Winter Jones's holiday absence, reported on the collection to the Trustees, recommending the purchase if Mr Stevens felt disposed to make a discount of one-third. The Trustees acceded to this proposal, and

and I was so informed, but instead of accepting it, the entire collection was withdrawn.

It had been so long on my hands, and this class of books was increasing so much in value, that I felt justified in adding twenty-five per cent to my prices and sending the whole collection to Mr Brinley. He promptly jumped at the lot, except a few that he possessed already in as good copies. These 'Mathers' constituted about two-thirds of the extraordinary Brinley collection sold in March 1878, for prices generally ranging from two to five times the prices he paid me some ten years earlier. It was a great gratification to me to find that in many instances both Mr Lenox and Mr Brown were the winners of these little nuggets that they had years before missed the opportunity of securing. It patted my poor judgment on the back, though perhaps a little late.

In books I found myself more of

an authority than in painting, sculpture, antiquities, etc. Early in 1847 I had an opportunity to secure what I believed to be a genuine full-length portrait of Washington by Stuart. I bought it, and took it to Boston with me the following November. It was exhibited, written about and talked about, but everybody discredited it; why I could not tell. My price was $1,000, but no body and no institution would buy it. Mr Lenox had nibbled at it and made inquiries about it through some one in Boston, but finally declined it. One day in the autumn of 1848, while gossiping with him, he inquired if I had sold my Stuart's Washington. I said 'No, nor can I account for its not going off at my reasonable price. Will you tell me frankly the reason you do not take it?' 'I do not mind telling you,' said he, 'if you will not be angry. It is because it is *yours*, and you cannot give its pedigree. You do not profess to be a connoisseur

seur in portraits, and your price is too low for a genuine Stuart.' 'I thought as much,' I replied. 'I am not angry, but only pity those who hang their art judgments on so slight a peg, and even that not their own.'

Mr Lenox subsequently bought a Stuart like mine, but with a pedigree, and mine, after eighteen months exile in its own land, found its way back to London, where it occupied for a few months my apartments at Morley's. I next offered it as it stood to Mr Russell Sturgis for £150, resolving to dabble no more in fine arts that required so much 'faith' in their owner, and 'push' in the seller. Mr Sturgis said he would gladly have it, if our friend Mr C. R. Leslie, R.A., who was well up in Stuart's work, would examine it and give his opinion that it was a genuine Stuart and all right. Accordingly Mr Leslie came and carefully examined the portrait, and not only pronounced it a good portrait but a good Stuart, and told me me unhesitatingly that he should by all means recommend Mr Sturgis to secure it at any reasonable price. I told him that it had become an elephant on my hands, and that being only too glad to get rid of it, I had offered it for £150, and then told him my fine art experiences. 'My dear sir,' said he sympathetically, 'had you asked £500 for it you would no doubt have sold it readily. Collectors are suspicious of low prices.' The picture was at once transferred to the right place where it is now fully and properly appreciated.

XIX

XIX

Mr Lenox declines the Large Paper Dedication copy of Smith's Virginia, also Gosnold's Voyage and Weymouth's Voyage, but afterwards buys them at the Brinley Sale

MR LENOX was very much interested in the bibliography of Captain John Smith's History of Virginia, and spent much time and a great deal of money in running out its history and variations, especially in the maps and plates. As early as 1852 we had a brisk correspondence for many months, and I procured for him a great many variations of the maps, and informed him of others in the

libraries

libraries of London, Oxford and Cambridge. The results of this correspondence were worked up by him in a paper entitled 'Curiosities of American Literature. No 1. Smith's General History of Virginia, New England and the Summer Islands,' which appeared in Norton's Literary Register in 1853 or 1854, signed L. In this he aimed at giving an account of all the mechanical features of the volume, together with all the known editions or variations of the maps, and a brief enumeration of the other works by Captain Smith: altogether, for a first attempt, a most valuable contribution to the bibliography of American History. A few copies were printed separately on blue writing paper. Eight distinct issues of the map of New England were described.

No 2 of the 'Curiosities' was a reprint of No 1, greatly enlarged, modified, corrected and improved, mostly based on the friendly criticisms

cisms and help of Dr Charles Deane. Both of these papers Mr Lenox subsequently sent to me with his manuscript additions and corrections, soliciting further criticism. I was able to send him several other items of interest generally, and particularly to raise the number of issues of the New England map to eleven.

Here the matter rested for several years, until the 1st of March 1873, when I wrote him:—'One should never despair. All rare books turn up sooner or later in London. Some twenty-five years ago you ordered or inquired about a large paper copy of Smith's History of Virginia. I offered £100 for Colonel Aspinwall's copy [then for sale], though broken in the binding, and two or three of the maps were supplied from a small paper copy. . . . That copy I had put in order by Bedford for the Colonel, and it is now the gem of Mr Barlow's collection. BUT, a few days ago, THE copy turned up in the library of a a clergyman in Yorkshire, lately deceased, the Rev Mr Lowe, brother of the Chancellor of the Exchequer. It is not only large paper, but is in the original binding in dark green morocco, very richly tooled all over, and in excellent preservation. It is the *Dedication* copy, and no doubt belonged to the Duchess of Richmond and Lenox. The Richmond and Lenox arms, very large and elaborate, with her quarterings, are on the side. The binding alone is, I think, the finest I ever saw of Charles I's time, and would readily bring £100 without the book. I am having it put in a morocco case, and shall next week send it out to [my agents] Messrs Austin, Baldwin & Co. Bankers, 70 Broadway. . . . I shall instruct them to give you the first offer, and if you decline it they are to send it at once to Mr Brinley. The price of the Smith is 250 guineas, a large sum for a Smith; but when you see the book I trust you will not think—or

rather

rather will think it not best to pass it.'

I had three weeks before, on the 8th of February, written to Mr Brinley, when sending him the Gutenberg Bible of 1450-55, and added this:—'The greatest bibliographical rarity that ever crossed the Atlantic ocean I shall send to Mr Lenox next week, but as he is only a millionaire and has stopped buying, he may not keep it at my price. In that case I shall direct Baldwin & Co to send it for your inspection. I trust your chances are small. I had the order from Mr Lenox twenty years ago, and am only now able to execute it; but I am more than rewarded for waiting, though the price of the book has gone up, while money has gone down. The book is Smith's History of Virginia on *large paper*, in the finest possible condition, bound at the time, 1624, in rich morocco tooled all over, with the arms of Charles on one cover and those of the Duchess of Richmond and Lenox on the other. In short, it is the Dedication copy to the Duchess, her own copy, in the most sumptuous binding, early English, I ever saw. Any book, no matter what, in such early English binding, would readily bring 100 guineas, but when that book is Smith's Virginia with all this story attached to it, and only five other large paper copies being known, and four of them in public libraries, what must I ask for this, THE copy of all others—a show book for ever, I think—but you must wait.'

Again on the 22nd of March, in a letter to Mr Brinley, I added :—'Mr Lenox writes me for the twenty-fifth time that he no longer buys books, and in his last letter has ordered nothing. So it is possible he may hold to this resolution until he has had time to pass the SMITH. If he does pass it, he is more of a . . . . than I ever took him for. However, you come in for the reversion of it if he does.' The book left Liverpool by the

the Cunard steamer March 15, only four days before the ill-fated 'Atlantic' sailed on her last voyage. On the 26th April I wrote :—'Baldwin of New York called on me this morning, and gave me the first information I had received respecting the Smith's Virginia. He said Mr Lenox called on him just before he left and told him that he had decided not to be tempted to buy any more books at present, and declined to trust his eyes to see it . . . I am not surprised at Mr Lenox passing the book judging from his recent letters, especially as he did not trust himself to see it . . . but his love of books is so big that he has to treat his good resolutions every little while and indulge.'

So the Smith became Mr Brinley's at about $1,275, but after his death it became eventually Mr Lenox's, by purchase at the Brinley sale in March 1878, Part I, No 364 at $1,800, or above 40 per cent advance on my price. In 1884 a similar copy, in the

the last Hamilton sale, wanting the large map of Virginia, brought £605, or about $3,000, which has also I understand found its way to New York, making three large paper copies in that city. The five copies in England known to me are the Grenville, Cambridge University Library, Lambeth Palace, Eton College and Mr Christie-Miller's. All this is I know mere bibliographical gossip interesting only to those far advanced in book-hunting, but it is for such these trivial matters are written out. On my congratulating Mr Lenox on his recovery from his non-purchasing resolutions, and his courage in so far topping my prices, he merely remarked that if I added simple interest for the five years to my price I would see that he had not paid anything more by waiting. To this I rejoined that I always supposed that the pleasure a millionaire derived from book-hunting more than paid the interest on his outlay.

Notwithstanding Mr Lenox's virtuous

tuous abnegation as to purchasing any more nuggets, I kept constantly supplying him with dainties, though more and more rarely. Sometimes however in a letter positively declining any longer to be tempted he would add a postscript inquiring after some lost lamb that I had offered him months before, and asking me if still on hand to send it to him. So I never felt quite disposed to cease offering him the choicer historical nuggets. Accordingly in the spring of 1874, having come into possession of fine large copies of Gosnold's Voyage to New England in 1602 by Brereton, and Waymouth's Voyage in 1605 by Rosier, I ventured to offer them to him as the 'Verie two eyes of New England History' for 250 guineas, but he let them also pass into Mr Brinley's hands. But at the Brinley sale he thought better of it and bought the two, March 11 1878, for $1,600, or nearly thirty per cent extra for waiting. See a full description of them

them in Brinley's sale, Part I, No 280. Mr Lenox was not however so lucky as to be able so easily for an advance to recover all the historical gems he had let slip through his fingers through a pardonable lack of prompt bibliographical appreciation and courage.

XX

The Vermonter burks a knockout. Mr Lenox declines more important 'Nuggets'

ABOUT 1852 my old friend William Pickering, one Saturday afternoon, showed me a catalogue he had just received of Lord Mountnorris's Library to be sold at Arley Castle the following Tuesday, and intimated that we might perhaps indulge ourselves in some rare sport in burking a projected knockout among the London booksellers, of which he had got wind. This suited my complexion, but it was necessary for us to know all about the books and their condition,

tion, and it was impossible for him to get away from town just then; so it was arranged that I was to see Messrs Farebrother & Co. the auctioneers, and obtain an order from them to examine the books on Sunday in time to set our traps for Tuesday.

Accordingly with the necessary order in pocket I telegraphed to a jobmaster in Birmingham to have a man and dogcart meet me at the station there on the arrival of the midnight train to take me over to Arley Castle some dozen miles. It was a fearfully rainy night, but we reached the little inn near the Castle before dawn, after a bibliographical steeplechase that ought to be celebrated in the annals of book-hunting. The next morning early, after a two hours' sleep and an hour's breakfast, I tried in vain as a casual to gain admission to the Library with proper assistants, until finally I produced my order with a sovereign wrapped in it. These brought two caretakers up smiling

smiling and we went not exactly to 'work' but to bibliographical devotion.

During the day I saw every book and every parcel, both printed and manuscript, and entered in my catalogue a rough estimate of the value of every lot. Before the sun set I set out for London by the Great Western route and was able to join Mr Pickering Monday morning with all the necessary information cut and dried for our purposes. We retired and went thoroughly through the numbers, fixing a low limit on every lot that we did not want, and a higher one on those lots we desired to secure. Mr Craven, Mr Pickering's accountant, was then called in and instructed. He left for Arley that night fully equipped and primed for battle. He was to procure, if possible, about a hundred lots. If the combined trade seemed disposed to let him have these lots at reasonable prices he was to bid on no others, but if they 'ran' him,

him, he was then without any bargain or compromise to bid on every lot up to a limit of about two-thirds of its market value which was marked in cypher in his catalogue. On his declining to join them the Philistines began to run him hard, but in every case he won *his* lots though at a high cost. He then began to play at their game and bid on every lot, but let them have all he was not told to secure. This spoiled their beautiful knockout, so that their dividend among above twenty hardly paid for their grog.

Our bill was large and on the whole not at extravagant prices. Among the books were many rarities for Mr Lenox. I took nearly the whole of Mr Pickering, allowing him a commission of ten per cent. Among the manuscripts which I secured were three which gave me infinite satisfaction, but I failed utterly for the next year or two to find any one else to appreciate them. They were, 1st, the

the original autograph manuscript, entitled 'A particular discourse concerning the greate necessitie and manifold comodyties that are like to grow to this Realme of Englande by the westerne discoveries lately attempted, written in the yere 1584, by Richarde Hakluyt . . . . at the requeste of Mr Walter Raleigh before the comynge home of his two Barkes [from Virginia, under Amidas and Barlow]' in 63 large closely-written folio pages; and, 2nd, two of the original autograph log-books of Capt. Luke Foxe's famous voyage in 1633 to Hudson's Bay.

These were all offered in May and June 1853 to Mr Lenox, Mr Brown, the British Museum, etc., but without any luck. Finally in 1854 they were thrown into auction at Messrs Puttick & Simpson's, and were bought by Sir Thomas Phillipps at prices nearly equal to what I had asked. Some years later when Dr Woods came over to seek for original historic materials

materials on behalf of the Maine Historical Society, I called his attention to this Hakluyt MS. He had it transcribed, and it was carefully edited and published as one of the volumes of the Maine Historical Society's Collections, a book of inestimable value on the origin and history of 'Western Planting' by the English Nation.

This was one of my many bibliographical failures, but I have never regretted my Saturday night and Sunday's experiences in that Arley book chase. If I made mistakes in the venture they were not so great as those of the gentlemen and librarians who declined to take the MSS. off my hands. I was equally unsuccessful in offering several other unique nuggets to Mr Lenox and others, which have remained unique to this day, as far as I know, such as 'The Temple of Wisdom,' or Withers' Abuses Stript and Whipt; with Bacon's Essays, printed by Bradford at

Philadelphia

Philadelphia in 1688, finally sold to Mr Menzies for 15 guineas, and the original 'Line of Demarcation' Bull of Alexander VI dividing the Indies between Spain and Portugal, printed at Rome in 1493 and dated May 4. Also a large block-leaf printed about 1499 or 1500 representing the Manners and Customs of the Natives of America, described fully with a not very clear fac-simile in my 'American Bibliographer No 1 1854,' and in my 'Historical Nuggets' No 77 £12 12*s*: sold at auction by Puttick & Simpson at a sale of some of my books, May 18 1854 (No 27 America) and bought in by myself in the name of Marchant for £3 13*s* 6*d*. It was again sold by me at Puttick & Simpson's March 6 1861 No 57 described as before, and was bought by C. J. Stewart the eminent Theological Bookseller for fifteen guineas. In 1866 the learned Henri Harrisse under his No 20 B.A.V. assigns the possession of it to the British Museum, and in in 1885 Mr Justin Winsor in his 'Narrative History' informs the world with his usual accuracy that 'the only copy known was bought in London at auction by the British Museum for £3 13*s* 6*d* in 1854.'

On enquiry at the British Museum in October and November 1885, no trace of this remarkable block-leaf could be found, and the librarians notwithstanding this cumulative evidence do not think the leaf ever found its way into the Library. I am unable now to trace this leaf on account of the death of Mr Stewart and the discontinuance of his business.

Another instance was the Second Bay Psalm Book of 1647, in 16mo, sold to Mr Brinley for $500, and resold in his sale Part I No 850 for the same price, the only other copy known being in the Library of the British Museum. Then there was Franklin's 'Liberty and Necessity,' London 1725, bought for 2*s* 6*d*, offered to the British Museum with its

its story for one guinea and declined on account of price, then offered to Mr Brown and Mr Lenox at five guineas and declined by both; subsequently thrown into auction at Messrs Puttick & Simpson's with nearly a half page note, where it fetched 19 guineas and was bought by Mr Hotten against the British Museum; on Mr Hotten's death in 1872 it was sold again by Puttick & Simpson for £22 10*s* again against the British Museum. Neither the Museum nor Mr Brown nor Mr Lenox ever secured this rare little book. My own copy (for I had a duplicate) is now slumbering in the 'Stevens Franklin Collection' in the Department of State at Washington, bought by the United States Government in 1881 for £7,000, in which I had valued it at £100. It is rather remarkable that both of the only two copies now known out of the 100 that Franklin printed himself at Palmer's at the age of 18 should have thus passed through my hands.

XXI

XXI

The Burns Autograph Manuscripts of 'Auld Lang Syne' and 'Scots wha ha' wi' Wallace bled.' Books in the Indian Languages

AFTER Mr Pickering's death I bought the better part of his collection of original manuscripts of Robert Burns, among which were the Autographs of 'Auld Lang Syne' and 'Scots wha ha' wi' Wallace bled'—two gems that I thought would be better appreciated in America than even in Scotland. But I again found that Mr Lenox's notion of their value did not tally with my own. So after keeping 'Auld Lang Syne' four or five

five years I sent it in 1859 by Capt Judkins to New York, to be expressed by him to Albany to be in time for the Burns Centenary Festival there. Chancellor Pruyn had written me about this proposed festival and asked me to send him in time for it something startling. I proposed that 'Auld Lang Syne' should be sung in Albany from Burns' Autograph, but there was not a moment to spare.

A railway guard by first train from London Saturday morning undertook to deliver the package personally into the hands of Judkins on the 'Russia' who had by telegraph been advised what to expect, and he was requested to use his best efforts to have it delivered to the train conductor to Albany as soon as he reached New York. In this way the Song reached Albany at nine o'clock in the evening and was delivered into the hands of Chancellor Pruyn, who at once interrupted the after-dinner speechmaking, and displaying his parcel requested all present to rise, join hands and sing 'Auld Lang Syne' from the poet's own handwriting, just received from London without an hour's delay. The effect was sublime, and the Chancellor thought this acquisition cheap at ten guineas and thanked me too.

The story of 'Scots wha ha'' was equally interesting. It was written on a single half sheet of quarto writing paper, and cost me at auction £33. This purchase by me was mentioned in the 'Times.' A few days later my old friend David Laing of Edinburgh wrote me that some years ago the papers of the Earl of Buchan, the correspondent of Washington, fell into his hands, among them a letter from Burns with the 'Battle of Bannockburn' attached, but the poem had been detached, and he never could hear of it. 'Now I suppose you have the one leaf and I the other. Pray send me the poem and I will send you many others in exchange.'

My

My reply was a letter inclosing half a dozen of Burns' poems and letters, and requesting him to send in exchange his letter to Buchan; 'for the two ought to come together again, never to be separated, and then to go to America where they would be so highly appreciated.' By return Mr Laing sent me the letter and I had them neatly joined and bound in a limp red morocco cover. This done, with patriotic pride and much pleasure, I reported the beautiful little volume to Mr Lenox at fifty guineas, with scarcely any advance on the costs. He declined it as too dear.

For nearly twenty years I retained it as an interesting autograph with which to astonish and out-brag my friends, frequently offering it to libraries and collectors at the fixed price, but found no one to admire it to the extent of fifty guineas, till my old friend Charles Sumner came and spent a morning with me during his last visit to London. Said he, 'I have bought

bought to take home with me one or two good engravings from Colnaghi, an old book or two from Quaritch, some old wine from Bond Street, and now what striking relic that I can buy and leave behind me can you suggest?' I showed him my Burns and told him its story, with its price, 'the rejected of men.' 'What! Mr Lenox, a New York son of a Scotchman, a collector and a millionaire, decline that for a paltry half-a-hundred guineas! I had rather possess this "Scots wha ha'" than anything else of the kind I can name.'

So Charles Sumner by exchanging a paltry cheque for fifty guineas on Barings became the owner of what he reckoned, during the short remainder of his life, the pride of his mementos and memorials of the great, and bequeathed it with the pomp of circumstance to the Library of Harvard College, where it now rests 'A thing of beauty and a joy for ever.' The poor thing, like many other of my my antiquarian and historical bantlings and pets, had eaten its head off, but I loved and cherished it as the bookmiser does his books.

In 1852 I had acquired a large and valuable collection of the rarest and earliest books in the Indian Languages of America. A full list with prices and bibliographical descriptions and collations was prepared, and the whole offered to Mr Lenox. He promptly declined nearly the whole as too dear, and added moreover that he had not made up his mind to invest in that class of Americana.

Mr Brown shortly after came to London and the collection was shown to him. It attracted his attention very powerfully, but never having bought many books of that class, he began to diplomatize and delay, taking time to make up his mind, but manifesting a strong desire to possess the whole. He however, after nibbling three or four weeks, finally said that he was going off to Paris and I need not reserve

serve the *dear* little volumes for him. When he returned, perhaps he might treat for them, but I was not to reserve them for him. Scarcely had he turned his back for France when Dr Cogswell showed up, with his grand new Catalogue, not of the Astor Library, but of the chief books he intended to buy for the Astor Library. He saw this linguistic collection, and though not one of the books was named among the 100,000 volumes of his future library, he pounced upon the whole like an eagle ever wide-awake and ready for his prey. He swept the board without any haggling about the prices. The volumes went to the Astor Library and Mr Brown never ceased mourning that lost opportunity. I am not sure that Mr Lenox ever manifested any particular craving for American linguistics.

XXII

XXII

Mr Lenox's method of recording his books. His failing health. The Stevens Catalogue of the Lenox Library proposed

IN 1855, when Mr Lenox was in London before going to the Continent, he came to my house every day for nearly a month, and we spent from 10 till 4 o'clock going over by divisions all my stock of Bibles and books relating to America, he pronouncing his decision, yes or no, on every one with remarkable promptitude and discrimination. At the same time, we went over together all his many notes of desiderata and imperfections. He collated

collated very carefully every book he bought, and then entered it or ticked it off in some class catalogue, or interpolated a brief manuscript record of it. The catalogues he used were mainly, for Bibles, Lea Wilson, Cotton, Ebert and Pettigrew. For books on America, Asia and Africa, he used Rich and Ternaux-Compans with MS. additions. These, together with his astonishing memory for details, for a long time enabled him to steer clear of duplicates, and to keep a comprehensive grasp of his accumulations. But it was overloading his memory and taxing cruelly his brain and health.

The amount of labour he performed in this way was prodigious, and it was all his own. No one was permitted to assist him. As he took up subjects and worked them out by study, correspondence or otherwise, he recorded the results in these temporary catalogues. The labor was absorbing and immense. No doubt

in

in time and in turn he would gladly have taken up many of the subjects and items I reported or submitted to him, but he was pre-occupied and so lost many an opportunity that occurs to a collector but once in a lifetime. The wonder is not that he missed so many chances, but rather that he missed so few of them.

On my arrival in New York at the beginning of September 1868, I found Mr Lenox despondent over the burden of his catalogues. There were many signs of his breaking down under their weight. His memory began already to fail to tell him where particular books were deposited, and it was not always easy for himself to find his brief record of them, nor was it possible for anyone else to find either the books or the entry of them. Under these circumstances our conversation was soon and naturally led up to a new and complete catalogue, in a single alphabet, of his entire library. I offered to make it

 for

for him, in the highest style of scientific bibliography in my power, and on my own responsibility, but under his supervision. He eagerly entertained the idea, but was exceedingly suspicious of the details and the possibility of carrying them out without great personal inconvenience, and bottomless risk to his books and manuscripts.

Now that these stores of historical and literary nuggets had become *his*, and were safely locked in his own closets, he seemed to forget that a very large portion of them had been *mine* for months or even years; collected and kept in my possession, collated, completed, bound, described, and reported to him with paternal care and perfect safety. However, after many interviews and much discussion for some six weeks as to the kind of catalogue to be made, and as to how, when and where the work could be done, I finally on the 18th of November reduced the results of our deliberations,

liberations, together with my own notions, to writing and handed him my first rough sketch of the proposed catalogue of the 'Lenox Library.' Two days later he wrote that my scheme brought 'the matter before him in a more definite shape.'

We continued almost daily to discuss the details of our plans, so that in a week he wrote, transmitting to me 'a sample of titles down to Ternaux No 100,' and intimated that if this sample suited my purpose he could go on as he had time. On my telling him that his method, as long as it omitted nothing as far as he went, was all I required for making my preliminary alphabetical list, he set to work with trip-hammer earnestness and speed, and in the course of less than six months supplied me from time to time with a brief but sufficient indication of nearly all the departments of his library, both printed and manuscript. During this time he was occasionally very ill from over-

over-work, and in his letter of May 10 1869, he wrote, 'My physician forbids my talking. The catalogue must I fear bear the blame.' He finally broke down, and was obliged to go into the country.

From Yonkers 19 June he wrote, 'You spoke, I think, of coming back in the late autumn or winter; and I would rather you should do so.... I feel that any thing attempted now would be done in a hurry, and certainly prove unsatisfactory. I must therefore stop here, and now.' I had by this time received his memoranda or notes of his entire Americana in all languages, his Miltons, his Bunyans, his Shakespeares, his Voyages and Travels, his Bibles, etc. etc. Under these circumstances, instead of returning as proposed to London, I decided to sit down in Boston and New York for a few months, and reduce my life-long observations into shape by studying into the 'Age of Discovery,' and especially into the

bibliography

bibliography of the early voyages of Columbus, Vespucci, and the first explorers of the new hemisphere. My papers on Tehuantepec and the Cabots were some of the results in the shape of Geographical Notes. I had previously put into type, privately in London, some 400 pages of bibliographical research respecting early Bibles in all languages.

XXIII

XXIII

The Stevens' Catalogue agreed upon and commenced. Correspondence on the subject

IN the course of the autumn of 1869 Mr Lenox's health and strength were such that he resolved to shift his burden by seeking an Act of Incorporation of 'The Lenox Library,' and transferring all his collections to the public. Early in 1870 this Act was passed, and the next time I saw him he exclaimed, 'Well, you now see what your doings have brought about! I was obliged on account of my health to wash my hands of the whole concern. Now, about our

our catalogue?' We had much correspondence and many interviews, until finally, on the 31st of May, I handed him duplicates of a letter I had drawn up, setting forth the plan of the proposed catalogue as far as we could settle it, including estimates of the cost in every particular. To this the same day he replied in duplicate; the two letters thus forming an agreement between Mr Lenox and me for a complete and elaborate printed catalogue of the Lenox Library. This agreement, together with a selection of the correspondence preceding it, is printed in small type below.

Clarendon Hotel, New York,
Nov. 18 1868.

To James Lenox, Esq. 53 Fifth Avenue.—Dear Sir,—You wish a catalogue of your library. I am willing to undertake it at once, and bring to bear upon it the results of my study and experience for the last 25 years. As I am now more free than I have been for a long time, or expect to be for the future, it will suit my convenience better to discuss the

the matter with you now than to defer it. If therefore you are disposed to treat with me I think we can settle matters one way or the other very speedily. No doubt we should readily agree upon the main points of a good common-sense alphabetical catalogue made with the highest degree of accuracy, of collation and description, with all the improvements of the latest and best bibliography. I do not know that I have quite determined upon what to call the best scheme of arrangement, or the precise style of printing, but as each book would be catalogued on a slip by itself, all these details might be settled when the MSS are nearly done, and we have the bulk of our copy before us. The catalogue would necessarily be in several parts or divisions, such as Bibles, Books on America, Voyages and Travels, Miscellaneous, etc., but I think it would be best to prepare the copy for the whole before any part goes to the press.

The *modus operandi* that would best suit me would be to go through your library at once, within the next two months, and make on small slips a very brief one-line schedule, generally under the headings the books would appear in in a general alphabetical catalogue. This work could I think be sufficiently well done in two or three weeks, and would enable us to have the whole subject fairly before us. I would then return to London,

say

say in January 1869, arrange the slips alphabetically, or in classes, as found most convenient, and print off, say half a dozen copies in a very condensed form for our own private use. This could cost very little. The titles would be numbered, and as you would have copies before you, all our correspondence would be by numbers. This done I could at once begin to look out all the titles and notes that I have accumulated during the last 25 years, and work them up with the aid of the British Museum and the Bodleian. In this way I could, I think, prepare seven-eighths of the titles better than I could possibly do them here, and have them ready by the end of next summer. I would then come to New York and apply my work to your particular copies, revise the titles with you, compare notes, settle discrepancies, and finally edit and prepare the manuscripts for the press. This I think we could do in three months hard labor. When the MSS. of the entire library are completed and we have compared and settled all our researches, I would again return to London and put the work through Whittingham's hand-press as fast as possible, keeping in your hands about 100 pages of proof all the time and printing off the sheets as fast as you could pass them. This plan at present would best suit me, and would give you, I think, the least amount of trouble, but if a better or more expeditious plan could be devised, I should of course be glad to adopt it. The work, if I go into it, would be done *con amore* and not for mercenary profit. Still I must live, and should expect a moderate remuneration in money. I would suggest that I should have also that part of the edition which will be for sale, but I am not disposed to drive a bargain. I wish to work up in the best form my accumulated materials in history and bibliography. I suppose therefore I ought to assume the responsibility of the work and place my name on the title-pages.

I will not to-day trouble you further. Pray take these as preliminary hints for consideration and discussion. If you on reflection are inclined to proceed with the matter, I will meet you any day I am in town. I am obliged to run round the country a good deal within the next fortnight, but letters here, or at 62 Cedar Street, will reach me if I am away.

I am yours truly, Henry Stevens.

---

53 Fifth Avenue, 20 Nov. 1868.

Henry Stevens, Esq.—Dear Sir,—I have your letter of the 18th inst. in reference to a catalogue. It brings the matter before me in a more definite shape; but there is so much to be said upon the subject that I cannot undertake to write all I have to say. When you may be in town, let me know, and

and I will try to arrange some opportunity when you may be able to call and see me.

Yours very truly, J. LENOX.

Friday night, 27 Nov. 1868.

H. STEVENS, Esq.—MY DEAR SIR,—I send you a sample of titles down to Ternaux No 100. It is not as neatly done as I should desire : but will it suit your purpose? If it will, I will go on as I have time. I have just recollected that I have a list from which I could probably make out a list of Bibles, &c., in other languages than English : and of American Bibles the titles of those in my possession may be culled from O'Callaghan, of which I presume you have a copy. Had I your printed titles, I could cut them up and by placing one in each of the volumes to which it refers, those might be put on one side, and thus render the cataloguing of the others more easy. Yours very truly, J. LENOX.

---

10 Dec. 1868.

MY DEAR SIR,—I have nearly made myself sick by preparing the accompanying papers : viz. a list of MSS. and eight other portions of my library. I find it no light work. I return your list of German De Brys. I would like to see you some little time before the day fixed for your departure. If this matter is to go on, it must be brought into a more definite shape, and that cannot probably be arranged

ranged at one interview. On any morning except Monday, I might see you at about half-past 9 o'clock, *except* next week, when it would not be convenient for me that you should come on Friday or Saturday. If possible I should like you to give me notice on the previous morning. Yours very truly,

H. Stevens, Esq. J. Lenox.

---

53 Fifth Avenue, 16 Dec. 1868.

Dear Sir, ... When I next see you I have some suggestions to make of importance, before I can come to a decision as to *the plan* of the catalogue. When you come, please bring a copy of the estimate you read me the other day. I wish to consider it at leisure, that I may if practicable make up my mind before you go away, *as to the whole matter*.

Yours very truly, J. Lenox.

Henry Stevens, Esq.

---

53 Fifth Avenue, 9 Jan. 1869.

My Dear Sir,—I have your note of 5th Jan. I have nothing at present to say to you to take up your time. I wish however that you would give me timely warning when you shall have fixed upon the day of your departure. There are many matters which must be determined before a positive resolution to print can be arrived at, and they cannot be resolved in a hurry. I have finished the Bib. Américaine

Américaine and also the Bib. Asiatique et Africaine [of Ternaux-Compans] : the latter was comparatively an easy task. I shall now commence the Bibles, probably next week.

Yours very truly,

H. Stevens, Esq. J. Lenox.

[Extracts.] 15 Feb. 1869.

I have not been well. . . . . . I have not proceeded with my list [of Bibles] as rapidly as before, although I have nearly two copy books full for you, but have not got quite to the end of Lea Wilson. I must again say to you that all our arrangements must be made in person. It will not do to leave anything to be settled by letter. I wish to see exactly, as far as possible, what I am about to undertake.

---

30 April 1869.

Dear Sir, ... Your note finds me in bed where I have been since mid-day yesterday, and I cannot tell when I shall be up again and able to attend to business.

---

53 Fifth Avenue, 10 May 1869.

Henry Stevens, Esq.—My Dear Sir,—I have been able to leave my room to-day for the first time ; but it will not be in my power to see you this week. My physician forbids my talking. The cataloguing must, I fear, bear the blame. Yours very truly, J. Lenox.

Yonkers,

Yonkers, Westchester Co. 19 June 1869.

HENRY STEVENS, Esq.—DEAR SIR,—I was so busy before leaving the city, that I could not ask you to see me again. I wanted to examine your sketch of expense of catalogue in order to come to some definite arrangement, and to make a change before any expense had been incurred. It is not a matter that can be closed in haste. My sickness and absence from town have caused delay, and further delay must necessarily follow from these and other circumstances. I have determined therefore to defer the whole subject to a later time, when I am at home, and you have less to do. You spoke, I think, of coming back in the late autumn, or winter; and I would rather you should do so, and give yourself to this one matter; this could be arranged hereafter by letter. I feel that anything attempted now would be done in a hurry, and certainly prove unsatisfactory. I must therefore stop here, and now, ...

I am, dear Sir, Yours very truly,

JAMES LENOX.

[Bill] No. 9. In Senate, January 12 1870. Introduced on unanimous consent by Mr. Tweed—read twice, and referred to the Committee on Literature.—Reported favourably from said Committee, and committed to the Committee of the whole. AN ACT to incorporate the trustees of the Lenox Library.

74 Parker House, Boston, Feb. 10 1870.

MY DEAR SIR . . . Mr Murphy has just sent me 'N.Y. Senate Bill No 9, Jan. 12 1870,' the Act incorporating the 'Lenox Library.' It is short, clear, clean and comprehensive; but I cannot help mentioning my being at Hartford a few days ago with Mr Brinley. He said that Mr Lenox had at last like Samson brought the whole fabric down upon himself—meaning that the great meddlesome American public would be down upon you and worry you to death. He hoped, and so do I, you will be able to resist as heretofore, and keep matters within your own hands for a long time to come; but I fear your strength . . . .

Yours truly, HENRY STEVENS.

JAMES LENOX, Esq. 53 Fifth Avenue, N.Y.

New York, 11th February 1870.

HENRY STEVENS, Esq.—MY DEAR SIR,—Your letter of the 10th inst. is just received . . . . . If there be anything of the Samson about me, I think it is only this—that I pull down the edifice on others and yet escape myself. By the way, I would like to get, if such a thing exists, the regulations of the British Museum as to the kind of books given to general readers in the hall. Is an introduction required? Do they allow the use of pen and ink or only pencils? And what are the regulations as to reserved books? What

What is the character of these? Introductions are required, no doubt, but of what kind? I have the regulations in Paris, etc., and I have no doubt, at least I always felt that when employed with such works I was secretly watched, and I felt very well satisfied that I should be watched. But I am not aware that in London I was watched. Do you know anything on the subject? I note these things more as topics of conversation when we meet than as asking you to answer them at once. But I must close.

Yours very truly, J. Lenox.

Clarendon Hotel, New York,
May 31 1870.

My Dear Sir,—The imperial octavo descriptive catalogue, such as we have discussed for the year past, of your entire collection of books and manuscripts, in one alphabet, with historical, geographical, chronological notes and illustrations, with full indexes, I estimate will cost you, for best hand-made paper, printing (including corrections), illustrations and binding, at the rate of £600 per volume of 500 pages, everything in its way to be of the best style and quality, something in appearance like that of Lord Spencer, but superior in many points. The editions to be 300 copies on the regular paper; 50 copies on the finest and best Dutch paper; 24 copies on very thin opaque strong writing paper;

paper; 2 copies on pure white vellum; or 376 copies in all of 4 sorts or editions. My calculations are based on an estimate of 2,500 royal octavo pages, or 5 volumes, to cost £3,000 as follows: Composition and printing 2,500 pages, 5 vols, £1,250; paper made to order, small, folding in 4to, 240 reams, £400; binding 1880 volumes in half roan, uncut, £150; Printing and binding, say 25 copies of the proposed hand catalogue, say 12,500 titles, 1 line each, small type, thin paper, very close, £100; Corrections, foreign, difficult printing, reimposing for the large paper copies, say £100 per volume, £500; Illustrations selected by Mr Stevens, £500; expenses of correspondence and transcripts, etc. in distant libraries, for the whole, say £100, amounting to £3,000; for my services, for say two years, or more if necessary, including my present collection of *copy*, and work already done, £1,000, besides one half of each of the above-named four editions, the cost bills payable quarterly if desired, and my salary at the rate of £50 a month, beginning with April 1870, £1,000; amounting to £4,000.

Yours truly, HENRY STEVENS.

JAMES LENOX, Esq. 53 Fifth Avenue, N.Y.

---

53 Fifth Avenue, May 31 1870.

DEAR SIR,—Your letter of this date on the foregoing page states the result of our

 several

several conversations respecting the catalogue of the Lenox Library, which you have undertaken to prepare and print. This is to be considered as a *maximum* estimate of the cost of such a work, to be modified hereafter upon your arrival in England and consultation with compositors, printers, etc., and such reductions will be made and such alterations in detail as may be suggested hereafter. Your previous investigations and preparations for an American catalogue so called, and your experience in different smaller publications of the same kind, enable you to be more definite in your calculations and estimate, than if the undertaking were perfectly new to you.

According to our understanding (not expressed in your letter) the work will be put in form as soon as possible after your arrival in London, be carried on by correspondence and frequent communication between us; and in November next I shall expect you here to collate, compare and describe such of my books as will require a very minute examination, and to prepare for commencing the printing of the catalogue.

I hope that both our lives may be continued to bring this work to a conclusion. You have undertaken that it shall be, as far as lies in your power, a catalogue sought after by bibliographers and bibliomaniacs, and I have little doubt that you can render it, I will not say a perfect work *of the kind we contemplate*,

contemplate, but approaching nearer to perfection than those attempted by your predecessors.

It is with this hope that I have agreed to enter upon my part; and I think the conditions as expressed in your letter manifest that I have done so in a liberal spirit. And I say to you, what I think I may add without laying myself open to a charge of boastfulness or vanity, that few men having made such a collection as mine, know so much about it as I do. I only wish that I knew far more about my books than I do. I do not intend to place myself in this respect upon the same platform as that on which you stand; but I do hope to be in some degree helpful in the work.

My note however has stretched itself out farther than I expected, but you have not left me time to shorten it.

I am, dear Sir, yours very truly,

HENRY STEVENS, Esq. JAMES LENOX.

New York, May 31 1870. RECEIVED this day One Hundred and Fifty pounds sterling of James Lenox, Esq. on account of three months salary according to the written agreement. HENRY STEVENS.

Clarendon Hotel, New York,
May 31 1870.

MY DEAR SELF,—Please find enclosed a Bill

Bill of Exchange for £100, being the first 2 months salary from Mr Lenox, April and May. Now do turn over a new leaf and look at both sides of your money before you spend it. If you will take advice from any one, I am sure you will from me. Be prudent, be industrious, hold your tongue, and remember that close mouths catch no flies. Go ahead and carry out this great work for Mr Lenox, and especially for the world and yourself. You have the opportunity. Improve it, and in two years let the world of book collectors and bibliographers have the opportunity of improving their minds. The writer intends to embark on the 'Russia' to-morrow with Mrs Stevens his wife, and Master Harry his son bound for dear old England, after an absence of 21 months. . . . . . So good bye and good luck. Thine *own*,

HENRY STEVENS.

To HENRY STEVENS, Esq. G.M.B.
4 Trafalgar Square, W.C. London.

Liverpool, June 11 1870.

MY DEAR SIR,—We reached Liverpool this morning, all well. Hope to be in London and in harness on Monday. There is nothing new under the sun. Passing through *Islington*, one of the good streets of Liverpool, this morning, my eyes were attracted by a prominent sign in large gilt letters,

THE LENNOX PUBLIC LIBRARY.

Of

Of course I crossed the street and entered the Institution. It is on rather a small scale, but calling to mind the fact that 'tall oaks from little acorns grow,' I inquired most respectfully into its origin, history and statistics. The result is enclosed in the shape of the catalogue of this Public Library. It is in fact Mr J. Lennox's private library, held for the use of the public for a moderate remuneration. I told the librarian, an intelligent young lady, that there was about to be established an institution in New York, for the use of the public, to be called 'The Lenox Library.' She expressed great interest in the matter, and said that she should be glad to exchange catalogues. I told her that I would with great pleasure forward her catalogue [a 12° tract of about a dozen pages] to the founder of the New York namesake, but that I believe no catalogue of that American library had yet appeared. I did not enlighten her as to the difference between the extent, aims or objects of the two Institutions. I hope you will preserve this Liverpool catalogue and have it appropriately bound. In haste, Yours truly,

HENRY STEVENS.

To JAMES LENOX, Esq.
53 Vth Avenue, New York.

The foregoing correspondence has little use now, except as a memorial of of an important literary enterprise that was begun in earnest, but for some reasons which I found it impossible to comprehend, was never carried out. In June 1870 I returned to London, and worked like an infatuated slave, *con amore*, all through that summer, in reducing my bibliographical accumulations into working order, printing my 'Schedule' of some 1,500 nuggets in single long lines, as a sort of specimen of our preliminary '*one line*' catalogue, and putting up a sample sheet, to show my idea of types, style, page, illustration, paper, etc., with corrected estimates of the whole work.

This all done to my own satisfaction I returned to New York in the following November to resume the work over the Lenox books and manuscripts for the winter of 1870-71. On our first interview I found Mr Lenox unusually distant, grumpy and formal. He appeared pale, nervous, and I thought, for the first time

with

with me, a little cross, though exceedingly polite and yet not cordial. He was sorry to see me he said, because he felt sure that nothing on the catalogue could be done at present, or perhaps until the books could be got out and removed to the new library building, then in course of erection. 'Besides,' he added, 'I am afraid that you have so much other work on hand that you will be unable to give your attention sufficiently to the catalogue.' This was new and unexpected, so I let him do most of the talking, hoping that by this means his mind might soon clear itself. 'Furthermore,' said he, 'I have been dreadfully disappointed that you did not answer my several letters, to which I attached much importance.' To this I mildly replied that there surely must somewhere be a mistake, for I had certainly answered fully the three letters in question, and could show him my press copies of them; and besides, I had received a reply to one

one or two points in one of the long letters! To this he shook his head and smiled incoherently.

Fortunately for me, just at that moment, he had occasion to unlock and open a strong writing-desk between the front windows, when on pulling out a drawer a roll of thin papers fell to the floor. On picking them up he stared at them for some time; then putting his hand to his forehead, exclaimed mournfully and apologetically, 'Oh, my memory! here are your three letters: they were received of course, and I remember now having placed them there for special reference, but can remember nothing more about them.' Immediately Mr Lenox was his dear old self again, and we had a long and earnest talk about the catalogue and the 'Lenox Library,' but the painful result was that he could not make up his mind to let me go to work in his house. It would fidget him to death to leave anyone in the house, and

and he must go out sometimes. After many unavailing suggestions, I, fully appreciating his timidity and apprehensions, agreed to postpone this proposed work for the winter, or perhaps till he was able to have a room in the new library building fitted up to receive a part if not the whole of the books, so that I might work uninterruptedly and to advantage on the catalogue from the books themselves.

In the spring of 1871 I returned to London, and for many months proceeded with the great work as well as I could from my old materials and from books in the British Museum and elsewhere. But it was like painting portraits from dummies and models. Mr Lenox had paid me regularly my salary of £50 a month from April to September 1870, and then without any notice or explanation ceased remitting. Our correspondence however continued about books, special subjects, and the progress of cataloguing for more than two years, I frequently requesting him to let me know when he was ready to let me examine his books and adapt my titles. That time was constantly deferred, as the completion of the library building was delayed.

Finally, towards the end of 1873, when the catalogue ought to have been completed and printed, he wrote me that he supposed I had understood that he had abandoned the work for the present. He must have forgotten that he had never written me to that effect; but as I found that the impediments were exceedingly unprofitable to me, and that now even perfect success would be a pecuniary loss to me, I let the matter drop silently into the pool of oblivion. I dare say that Mr Lenox had some good reason for not proceeding with the catalogue, but if so he never acquainted me with it. However, my three years of 'posting up' my bibliographical studies were not all thrown

thrown away. My studies and business continued, and in 1877 I had the honour and pleasure of shunting a segment of my Bible bibliography, on very short notice, into my 'Catalogue of Bibles in the Caxton Exhibition.' Other portions of those accumulations are now (1885) being worked up, with my son, in the continuation of my 'Historical Nuggets.' Mr Lenox died in 1880, and the 'Lenox Library' is understood to be flourishing in New York, but the 'Stevens Catalogue of the Lenox Library' has never yet been resumed, though the agreement for the manufacture of it has never yet been cancelled.

THE END.

CHISWICK PRESS :—C. WHITTINGHAM AND CO.,
TOOKS COURT, CHANCERY LANE.

www.ingramcontent.com/pod-product-compliance
Lightning Source LLC
LaVergne TN
LVHW011202110826
845150LV00006B/1292
9781425572471